WIRED *for* DATING

How Understanding Neurobiology *and* Attachment Style Can Help You Find Your Ideal Mate

Stan Tatkin, PsyD, MFT

New Harbinger Publications, Inc.

D0008964

Publisher's Note

Distributed in Canada by Raincoast Books

Copyright © 2016 by Stan Tatkin
                New Harbinger Publications, Inc.
                5674 Shattuck Avenue
                Oakland, CA 94609
                www.newharbinger.com

Cover design by Sara Christian
Acquired by Tesilya Hanauer
Edited by Clancy Drake

FSC
www.fsc.org
MIX
Paper from
responsible sources
FSC® C011935

Library of Congress Cataloging-in-Publication Data

Tatkin, Stan, author.
  Wired for dating : how understanding neurobiology and attachment style can help you find your ideal mate / Stan Tatkin, PsyD, MFT ; foreword by Harville Hendrix, PhD, and Helen LaKelly Hunt, PhD.
    pages cm
  Includes bibliographical references.
  ISBN 978-1-62625-303-2 (pbk. : alk. paper) -- ISBN 978-1-62625-304-9 (pdf e-book) -- ISBN 978-1-62625-305-6 (epub) 1. Mate selection. 2. Dating (Social customs) 3. Sexual attraction. 4. Interpersonal relations. 5. Neurobiology. 6. Attachment behavior. I. Title.
  HQ801.T277 2016
  306.73--dc23
                         2015032698

Printed in the United States of America

18   17   16

10   9   8   7   6   5   4   3   2   1   First printing

"Bravo, Stan Tatkin, for writing a truly useful book about dating: what to look for; how to handle Internet dating sites; what to know about yourself; how to vet potential partners; and how to proceed in a level-headed fashion toward finding life's greatest prize—a long-term successful partnership. Moreover, it's got poetry, a grounded understanding of neuroscience and attachment theory, excellent questions and exercises, and really smart advice. I learned a lot. It's a special book."

—**Helen Fisher, PhD**, biological anthropologist at Rutgers University, chief scientific advisor to the Internet dating site www.match.com, and author of *Why Him? Why Her?*, *Why We Love*, *Anatomy of Love*, *The First Sex*, and *The Sex Contract*

"People entering into relationships today need this book more than ever. *Wired for Dating* goes beyond simply being a guide on increasing your chances of successful dating; Stan Tatkin, PsyD, provides a science-based approach filled with valuable insights and techniques that can give us the ability to create more enduring and richer relationships. This book can transform the culture we live in today!"

—**Elisha Goldstein, PhD**, cofounder of The Center for Mindful Living in Los Angeles, CA, and author of *Uncovering Happiness*

"Perhaps nothing is as pivotal in creating enduring and satisfying relationships as the intricate dance of dating. Stan Tatkin has found a way to make the complexities of this elusive process clear, without diluting the science and clinical practice that inform this central life issue. *Wired for Dating* is a flexible and supportive guide for those running the relationship gauntlet, as well as a significant contribution to emotionally based therapies."

—**Peter A. Levine, PhD**, author of *Waking the Tiger*, *Healing Trauma*, and *In an Unspoken Voice*

"The best step-by-step manual for how to conduct yourself on a first date, vet a prospective partner, and keep yourself from inadvertently destroying the relationship."

—**Dan Wile, PhD**, author of *After the Honeymoon*

"If you are thinking about starting to date, are excited about a person you recently met, or have met the love of your life, you will find reading this book an eye-opening experience. Stan Tatkin has succeeded in integrating attachment and neuroscience research as he takes us on a wonderful journey through the worlds of dating, mating, and love."

—**Marion F. Solomon, PhD**, author of *Narcissism and Intimacy* and *Lean on Me*

"Meeting and coming together with a mate doesn't have to be a happenstance affair. In *Wired for Dating*, Stan Tatkin lays out what you need to know and specifically what you can do to have the best chances of success in a relationship. Expert advice for people of all ages and all shades of prior experience who are serious about finding happiness in a lasting long-term relationship."

—**Bill O'Hanlon**, coauthor of *Love is a Verb* and *Rewriting Love Stories*

"Stan Tatkin's *Wired for Dating* is a wonderful, supportive guide to self- and relationship discovery. It is filled with nuggets of wisdom that make it easy to answer some of the toughest dating questions. Using Tatkin's psychobiological approach, you can navigate dating with much more grace. You have a way to identify serious red flags, as well as the exercises and skills to build a long-term successful partnership. Now you can choose a life partner with confidence and the clarity that you are right for each other. Reading *Wired for Dating* is one of the most important decisions you will make in your mating life."

—**Ellyn Bader, PhD**, cofounder of The Couples Institute
in Menlo Park, CA

"Stan Tatkin's marvelous and intelligent guide gives you the total map when you seek a partner worthy of your efforts and ask the important question, 'Is this the right one for me?' Tatkin shows you how to use both sides of your powerful brain and finally make the right decision. The heart meets science, and you're the winner. He takes the mystery out of dating so you can enjoy the mystery of being with the person you really love. Now you can date with a safety net, and enjoy the journey as the genuine magic happens."

—**Peter Pearson, PhD**, cofounder of The Couples Institute
in Menlo Park, CA

"Stan Tatkin is one of the most important voices in couple relationships today. His knowledge is grounded in research, packed with practicality, and sprinkled with a unique blend of wisdom and wit. Take the time to read *Wired for Dating*; you will be rewarded with inspiration and insight."

—**Pat Love, EdD, LMFT**, coauthor of *How to Improve Your Marriage Without Talking About It*

"Stan Takin is one of the leading figures in relationship counseling. In *Wired for Dating*, he explains partnership science so that readers can create a secure, meaningful relationship. Study this book before commencing your relationship journey so you have a map for success. Learn these methods when you are partnered to chart its continuation. Easy to read, eminently practical."

—**Jeffrey K. Zeig, PhD**, founder and CEO of The Milton H. Erickson Foundation

"Where was Stan Tatkin when *I* was dating? I highly recommend *Wired for Dating* to anyone who is ready for a secure-functioning relationship. Tatkin addresses the scientific, psychobiological, neurobiological, and intricate ways of the nervous system within the realm of dating, and does so in an utterly readable, practically applicable, wise, and entertaining way."

—**Alanis Morissette**, artist and activist

To my wife, Tracey, and daughter, Joanna,
who keep me going and loving life.

Contents

Foreword

Harville Hendrix, PhD and Helen LaKelly Hunt, PhD

Dating is a relatively recent social practice, with roots in the 1700s, when marriage by choice began to replace arranged marriages. In previous centuries, in most cultures, you could not vet your potential mate and you did not have to be attracted to or even like the person! You just had to marry him or her for the social and economic good of your family.

As marriage by choice gained popularity, the wisdom and intuition of elders—known as matchmakers—helped give potential mates more freedom and opportunity to meet and marry someone they liked. And with the matchmakers' due diligence, single people could more easily discover whether they were compatible economically and socially. In recent decades, social and economic compatibility have receded in importance, and personal compatibility has moved to the forefront. The contemporary "search and find" dating process makes use of casual meetings, recommendations by friends, participation in various clubs and groups, bar hopping, and, most recently, the Internet. Rather than relying on the wisdom and intuition of experienced elders, we now look to instinct, or our unconscious, to guide us in choosing a mate. The outcome has so often been so contrary to what the couples had dreamed that marriage is more generally associated with misery than with the euphoria of the dating period.

Now we are entering a new age of dating, where instinct, intuition, and wisdom are informed by a new relational science. Based on this science—as represented in this book—partner selection can be improved, preparing for marriage can hold the key to the marriage's success, and potential mates can make the radical new claim that a happy marriage is possible and its quality durable!

Relationship science gives us precise insight into the involvement of emotional development and neural functioning in partner choice, relationship quality, and relationship durability. This insight opens the door to a new future for marriage, and mitigates the historical split between the joys of courtship and the disillusionments of marriage. It also portends a future with a divorce rate much lower than 50 percent.

Wired for Dating intends to help individual readers use the dating process to develop a relationship that thrives and lasts. And while it was not the author's intention to posit a wider social vision, his description of a dating process that can lead to successful partner selection and a durable, happy, intimate, life-long monogamous relationship offers new hope for humanity. Stan Tatkin's value system and his knowledge that the connection between marital quality and societal health is causal are consistent with a vision of a new era of scientifically informed dating that portends the advancement of a new social order—a civilization of love.

We have been involved with couples work for three decades, writing books, doing therapy, and leading intensive couples workshops. Our vision has been a new possibility for intimate partnership that would make marriage attractive again, reduce the 50 percent divorce rate of the past sixty-five years, and improve the relational quality of our society. Included in that vision of a shift from conflict to connection is a policy change that would make taking a course on the science of marital happiness mandatory before the state issues a marriage license. There is an irony in the fact that driving a car or styling hair or repairing electrical circuits requires taking a long course and passing a test, whereas getting a marriage license—the most important life decision most of us ever make—requires only a few dollars and a pair of signatures. And neither course nor license is required to have a child. Something needs to change!

From our perspective, the problem lies in the value system of our culture. For two centuries, the protection, support, and promotion of the welfare of the *individual* as an isolated, autonomous, and independent self has dominated our cultural agenda. Relationship, perceived as both secondary in value and a derivative of the self, has been a casualty of this obsessive individualism: a relationship that does not provide happiness to the self is considered dispensable.

In *Wired for Dating*, Stan Tatkin turns the world agenda upside down when he asserts that self-love and self-interest are not, in fact, the starting points of a relationship. Citing the infant-caretaker relationship, he asserts that we are loved before we can love, and that self-interest is preserved and enhanced by interest in others. This challenges the myth of the primacy of the individual and replaces it with science-based evidence that we are, at our core, relational beings, and that our welfare is dependent upon our relationship with others. The reality that we are social beings is reflected neurologically by the fact that our brain requires interaction to grow, and that therefore the quality of our interactions determines whether our brains are healthy.

We are born in relationship. We are also wounded in relationship and healed in relationship, and we thrive only in relationship. We *need people* to thrive. The point cannot be made too strongly: relationship is primary reality; the individual self is a derivative. This is a paradigm shift of enormous proportions, and it can be facilitated by implementing the insights of the relational sciences prior to marriage, in dating practices. This book is more than a guide for aspiring couples; the application of its insights will affect the value system of the culture in a positive way.

Introduction

If you have picked up this book, chances are you are interested in finding a romantic partnership. This could take a variety of forms. It could be a traditional marriage, civil union, or some other form of long-term commitment. It could be heterosexual or same-sex. It may be more or less "romantic" in flavor. In fact, you may be uncertain about whether you believe in or are ready for a full commitment, yet yearn for greater companionship of some sort. Maybe you just want to test the waters and explore your options. In any of these situations, dating, the most common way we explore and form relationships in our society, is on the table—and likely on your mind.

In my work as a couple therapist and as the leader of workshops for people who are in a relationship or are interested in finding one, I am familiar with the full range of scenarios. For example, I often see people who wish to find a partner, but whose fears cause them to avoid intimacy. Others have been dating someone for a while but don't know how to determine if that person is right for the long term, or if they should cut bait and move on. Still others carry such strong hurts from prior relationships that they wonder if dating is worth the trouble. There are also individuals who have been away from the dating scene for decades and have been thrust into it again, and who wonder if they have what it takes to go through the process all over again.

Regardless of which of these examples is most like your own situation, dating can be a daunting prospect. It can be scary simply because you've never done it. Romantic images surround you, in books and movies and social media and in friends' lives, but it is something else to try to create all this yourself. Dating can also cause anxiety and frustration when you have been out there meeting people for what seems like forever without finding the right partner. You date person after person until you're so exasperated you're ready to quit. And dating can be intimidating and stressful if you've been out of the scene for years and no longer know how to go about it.

To be honest, when I was asked to write this book, my first thought was *Does the world really need another book on dating?* So much has already been said on the subject. Yet practically on a daily basis I meet people who are confused about how to create successful relationships. Despite all the information and advice out there, they are unsure how to proceed. They don't know how to correct mistakes they feel they've made. Instead of enjoying the prospect of dating, they dread it. Sometimes they question the fundamental reason for having romantic relationships.

I decided to write this book because I believe my approach to finding romantic relationships through dating offers something you won't find elsewhere. My approach is a *psychobiological* one. This means it uses science-based insights into both the psychological and biological aspects of romantic relationships. It draws on research from the fields of developmental neuroscience, attachment theory, and arousal theory

Neuroscience is the study of the human brain. Among other things, it provides a basis for understanding the physiology of how we act and react in relationships. For example, the most primitive, automatic parts of your brain play a large role in determining what attracts you to a potential partner. The more socially evolved parts of your brain, working in conjunction with the more automatic parts, allow you to do things—such as read faces, emotional tone, and social cues—that increase your chances of success on a date.

Attachment theory explains our biological need to bond with others. It helps us understand how, for example, the kinds of bonds formed during our earliest relationships set the stage for our basic sense of safety and security in later relationships. Some people are fundamentally secure in relationships, while others are insecure. Insecurity can make it more difficult for you to get close to a potential partner, or can cause you to feel ambivalent about dating in the first place. While you can't change your basic orientation with a snap of your fingers, styles of relating are not static. I will show you how to move toward greater security within a healthy relationship.

The biology of human arousal, or *arousal theory*, also provides us with good insights and tools for navigating dating and relationships. "Arousal" in this sense doesn't mean specifically sexual arousal, but rather the more general ability to manage one's energy, alertness, and readiness to engage. In the context of dating, this means you don't have to remain at the mercy of your moods and feelings. Instead, you can learn to manage your own feelings, and to influence, soothe, and inspire your partner.

In my book *Wired for Love*, I applied this psychobiological approach to people who are already members of a couple, to help them improve their relationships. The basic premise of that book is that we are naturally wired more for war than for love. Our insecurities and our inability to manage our moods and energy levels cause the part of our brain that is wired for war to prevail even when we wish it wouldn't. In *Wired for Love*, I offer a series of ten principles, along with supporting techniques and exercises, to help couples swing the pendulum toward love, so they can get what they really want from each other in relationship.

I'm excited now to be discussing a step that comes earlier in the relationship journey: dating. My thesis is that we have the power to swing the pendulum during the dating journey itself so we are better prepared to find a partner and successfully make a lifelong commitment.

Merriam-Webster defines *dating* as "the series of social engagements shared by a couple looking to get married." I think we can

3

agree this definition is too narrow to encompass all the reasons for dating in our modern world. At least for the purposes of this book, "dating" is something more along the lines of "the social process shared by people looking to form a secure-functioning relationship."

The central idea of this book is that secure functioning is at the core of all successful relationships. The principle of *secure functioning* is rooted in attachment theory and research, and describes a relationship with the following characteristics:

- Security ("we protect each other")

- Sensitivity ("we are aware of each other's needs")

- Justice and fairness ("we quickly repair any hurts that occur")

- Collaboration ("we're in this together")

- True mutuality ("what is good for me is good for you")

Thus, we say that partners in a secure-functioning relationship are grounded in sensitivity, fairness, justice, collaboration, and true mutuality. We all have the basic wiring for these characteristics, but we sometimes need to strengthen that wiring in order to offset any counter-tendencies.

Although there are many paths to success in relationships, this book is written primarily with the goal of helping you find a single, long-term, monogamous partner. For this, understanding and applying the principle of secure functioning are key. I'm going to teach you not just how to prepare yourself for dating itself, but for how to use the dating process to create a romantic relationship that is (or will become) secure functioning. I believe this approach is the most effective way to resolve the fear and frustration so many of us experience as we go through the dating process. The good news is that regardless of your own particular set of fears or hesitations or concerns, the ingredients of the solution are essentially the same.

I would sum up these ingredients in the following universally applicable psychobiological principles for dating. As you can see, they are consistent with the characteristics of secure functioning:

1. Dating partners keep each other safe and secure; even if they don't know each other well, they always protect one another.

2. Dating partners are aware of and responsive to each other's needs.

3. Dating partners move quickly to repair any hurts that occur in their new relationship.

4. Dating partners recognize they are in a process of joint exploration, and they help one another learn about each other.

5. Dating partners practice true mutuality; regardless of their individual styles of relating, they know that what is good for one is good for the other.

In essence, if you and a potential partner can practice these principles, you give your relationship the highest possible chance for success. Conversely, if you find a dating relationship does not embody these principles, you have good grounds for calling it quits and moving on.

This book is organized to roughly parallel the arc of the dating journey itself, starting in chapter 1 even before you go on your first date. In that chapter, I'll go into more detail about my approach to dating, and you will have a chance to consider various issues before you embark, such as the kind of partner and relationship you want, the pros and cons of online dating, and some common myths about relationships. This is not to say that you should skip this chapter if you are already dating someone. It is never too late to make sure you're clear about what you want.

Chapters 2, 3, and 4 move on to the first date or the first few dates. We look at what is really happening when you are attracted to someone, what you can do right from the start to begin to vet a potential partner, and what you can do to make sure you put your best foot forward. Again, even if you are already dating, these chapters contain valuable information and techniques you can apply at any stage of the game.

In chapters 5 through 8, we go more deeply into the dating process. This is when you start moving from casual dating to something more serious. This process can take approximately a year, so if you have not yet started to date, you will obviously be reading this with an eye to the future. Chapters 6 through 8 address issues encountered in each of the three main relationship styles—island, wave, and anchor; more about these later—and explore how partners with different styles can move toward secure functioning.

Chapter 9 expands upon the principles introduced in chapters 3 and 4. You learn both how you and your potential partner can soothe each other and how you can best deal with any conflicts that arise. At this point in a relationship, your journey can go one of two ways: you can break up or you can form a commitment. Chapter 10 considers the question of how to determine whether it is time to call it quits, how to handle a breakup if you feel that is inevitable, and how to recover as quickly and easefully as possible and move on. Finally, in chapter 11, I show you how to take your dating partnership to a new level, if you feel you are ready for that, and how to formulate a formal agreement with your partner that lays the foundation for a sound, lasting, and loving commitment.

Each chapter includes exercises, and I encourage you to do them. This book is about *you*, and the exercises are what really make it personal. Some exercises may seem more appropriate to you than others, depending on where you are in the overall dating process. So feel free to focus on some now and leave others for later.

As you read through the chapters in sequence, you will cumulatively gather the knowledge and skills you need to achieve your dating goals. I recognize that goals will vary depending on each reader's situation and his or her own internal wiring. For this reason, I have included cases that span the spectrum of dating possibilities so that hopefully you can find examples that speak to your current situation as well as learn from others that reflect a broader diversity of experience. By the final chapter, as you synthesize all the information, you should be well on your way to finding a partner with whom you can build a lasting relationship from the ground up.

CHAPTER 1

Before You Date

Bev, a flight attendant who has never been married, is at home for a week and sitting down for coffee with her younger sister, Dorothy. Before they've even added cream and sugar, the conversation turns to their usual topic: relationships.

Bev begins by announcing she has been using the online dating service Dorothy recommended. "I know it's working for you," she says. "But I'm not sure about me. I've been trying so long to find the perfect person that, at this point, I'm not sure anything could help—not to mention I turned forty last month."

"I'm a year older," Dorothy reminds her. She is now dating a man, divorced like herself, whom she met online.

"I'm happy for you," Bev says. "But what about that guy you met last year?"

Dorothy gives a nervous laugh. "Turns out he was married. He conveniently forgot to include the fact on his profile."

"I'm sorry." Bev shakes her head. "I've heard too many dating nightmares. Maybe I'll just stay single. I love my job, and life's not so bad."

Dorothy agrees the horror stories exist, but still thinks the risks are worth it. "Didn't you find *anyone* interesting?" she persists. "You wanted to find someone creative."

Bev responds by reeling off a list of men who responded, mostly artists and musicians. Because of her work schedule, she was only able to meet one. He was attractive, but she realized he was financially unstable.

"If we got together, I'd have to support him. Obviously that's not an option." A musician she spoke with came across as arrogant, and she sensed several others were really looking for younger women. She concludes by saying, "Maybe I'm too old to share my life with some-one. Besides, who says there's such a thing as a good marriage?"

If you're excited about dating, Bev's situation and her conclu-sions may sound a bit extreme. But I've included her story because I meet so many people—especially those who've been dating for a while—who have become overwhelmed and feel defeated. Some are ready to call it quits. Others are just setting themselves up for future failure. What these individuals have in common is that they are unclear about why they want to date, the kind of person they want to date, and the kind of relationship they wish to end up in.

The topics I'll cover in this chapter are all ideally ones to think about before you begin dating, to help you gear up for the process. However, even if you are actively dating, it's not too late to go back to basics and resolve any issues and concerns you still have. Or if, like Bev, you've come to a point of feeling your years of effort have been in vain, then please don't despair: there is hope! This chapter's exploration of relationship basics gives you a foundation on which to build.

We begin by looking at common assumptions people bring to the dating process, especially assumptions that can undermine their chances of success. I'll also go into more detail about the scientific principles that underlie the psychobiological approach, discuss the pros and cons of online dating, and dispel some myths about dating and relationships.

YOUR STARTING POINT

People have many reasons for dating: they may want to get married, start a family, avoid being alone, establish independence, expand their circle of friends, or seek new experiences. All these are valid reasons, but in this book I'm going to assume you want to date because you are serious about finding a committed partner. In that case, it's helpful to start by examining the ideas and preconceptions you have about the kind of partner, and kind of relationship, you want. Your ideas are what you bring to the table, and as such they play a role in determining where and with whom you end up.

I'm going to venture out on a limb by saying this: the chances are pretty good—whether you admit it or not and whether you are male or female—that you are looking for one special person, not two or three or more. Chances are also pretty good that you are seeking both some degree of relationship permanence and some degree of interdependency. At the same time, I would hazard a guess that you are wondering if this kind of committed relationship is possible for you. Even if you want to believe it is possible, you may wonder if it is really worth pursuing. Maybe you feel you're not "made" for relationships. Or you think pairing up is a trap you'd be smart to avoid. In short, like Bev, you may be experiencing a big dose of dating-and-relationship skepticism right about now.

There is a reason that seeking a partner isn't as straightforward as, say, going through the process of buying a new car or new house. When it comes to courtship, biological and social influences can be at odds. It may be that your biological hard wiring leads you to want a committed relationship, but that the prevailing mores in your social group carry a strong pull in the opposing direction. For instance, if you're a young person and your friends spend more time socializing in groups than dating, you are likely to do the same, regardless of other inclinations you may feel. Similarly, if you watch movies or TV shows in which multiple partners, or many partners in quick succession, are the norm, that may have an impact on your choices. These kinds of social trends can cast doubt on what you otherwise would consider the best way to form relationships. In the pages that follow, we will look more closely at this dichotomy.

EXERCISE: YOUR DREAM PARTNER

I've just shared a few ideas about what I believe drives people when they think about finding a partner. But what counts is what *you* want. The following ten questions can help you gain clarity on that, and that clarity can help keep you grounded throughout the dating process.

1. What is your ideal partner's appearance? Include age, gender, hair, height and weight, style of clothing.

2. Where or how do you think you are most likely to meet your ideal partner?

3. What are your ideal partner's main personality traits?

4. What is your ideal partner's prior relationship history?

5. What is your ideal partner's financial status? Occupation? Hobbies? Interests?

6. How would your ideal partner treat you? Treat others?

7. How much time would it take after meeting your ideal partner for your first kiss? Sleeping together? Living together? Engagement? Marriage? Children?

8. What would your ideal partner say or do first thing each morning?

9. What would your ideal partner give you on your next birthday?

10. How would your ideal partner react if the two of you had a disagreement?

You might want to write down your responses to these questions, or record them on your phone, so you can revisit them later, as you get further into the dating process. Be prepared for your answers to shift as you gain greater clarity about what you want in a partner.

PAIR BONDING

When I said I was going out on a limb by suggesting you're probably seeking a single special person, I wasn't saying anything particularly revolutionary. At most, it was a low limb on a short tree. In other words, when I say this, I have science on my side. In particular, the various scientific disciplines that contribute to a psychobiological perspective have a lot to say on this matter. Let's look at some of the facts and findings.

One relevant science-based fact is that humans are dependent animals. You might prefer to say that we are *inter*dependent, which sounds more appealing than "dependent." In fact it is more accurate because others also depend upon us. However, we don't start off as interdependent; we begin our lives dependent on another person to fulfill our every need.

Psychologist John Bowlby (1969) was one of the first to study the human tendency for *pair bonding*—that is, the formation of a close relationship between two individuals. He developed *attachment theory* to explain why we bond in pairs, starting with our very first relationship outside the womb. We cannot survive and thrive without that special relationship, which usually occurs with our mother. As we grow up, we are born into a larger-sized womb (the world). The initial bonding that began immediately after birth gradually delivers us into a world of increasingly larger numbers of things and people. But the fact that we started off as one person bonded with one primary other influences everything going forward.

Perhaps the most significant influence that initial relationship has is on how we form romantic relationships. As adults, ostensibly, we date because we want to be in a primary relationship with one other person. To be successful, that relationship needs to be reliable, safe, mutual, trustworthy, dependable, and rewarding. In other words, it needs to be secure functioning. Of course, some people did not have the benefits of safety and security in their first relationship. As a result, they may carry a fear—conscious or unconscious—of getting hurt again. The best way they know to protect themselves from another broken heart is to avoid getting too close to one person. They may think they want to find a partner, yet feel conflicted about doing so. The good news, at least from the psychobiological perspective, is that although the residue from early experiences can make the dating process more challenging, most people are able to go on and form secure and loving relationships. It just may require a bit more effort.

Biological and Cultural Imperatives

Human nature has provided human beings with a biological imperative to procreate and continue the species—an imperative some people feel more keenly than do others. We also all have a biological drive for skin-to-skin contact. Raylene Phillips (2013), who summarized research on the effect of skin-to-skin contact for newborns, tells us that babies who get enough early skin-to-skin contact have better physical functioning and more optimal brain development, and cry less. Similarly, we have a biological need for eye-to-eye and face-to-face contact. Psychologist Allan Schore (2002) has written extensively about the psychobiological necessity of eye-to-eye, skin-to-skin, and face-to-face contact for adequate brain development and for developing social-emotional skills and abilities. Again, some of us have a stronger need for this close physical contact than do others.

13

While nature has a plan for procreation, scientists have yet to identify a natural plan for long-term, committed relationships. This is generally considered a matter of culture, or if not culture, then of social survival. And cultural imperatives change. Thus, we see different reasons for forming long-term relationships in different parts of the world, and we see these reasons evolving over time. For instance, in past centuries, it was more common than it is today for people to marry for the purpose of combining properties and monies, or for social gain.

According to the Pew Research Center (Desilver 2014), love is the reason most (88 percent) of Americans cite these days for getting married. Also high on their list are making a commitment, and companionship (81 percent and 76 percent, respectively). Notably, 70 percent of Americans today say they are in a committed relationship, although only about 50 percent are married. If these statistics tell us anything, it's this: your desire to date is supported by the culture, albeit equivocally. By that I mean you probably grew up expecting to find someone special and spend the rest of your life with that person, but along the way you received some contradictory messages.

It can be tough if you are feeling under pressure to find a partner but view dependency as a weakness, or if you see marriage as an outdated institution. I don't think there is a quick solution for this kind of dilemma. Moreover, the solutions vary depending on your situation. If you are new to dating, resolving this issue may be part of your process of separating from your family and clarifying your own values. If you have a same-sex orientation, these issues may dovetail with larger social and political issues. If you are dating after the painful end of a long-term relationship, you may need to resolve feelings specific to that relationship first. In general, though, my suggestion is to allow yourself to temporarily live with any ambiguities related to your search for a partner. Again, hopefully you will be able to clarify these kinds of issues for yourself as you continue to read and to proceed with the dating process.

THE PSYCHOBIOLOGICAL BOTTOM LINE

So where does all of what I've said so far leave you?

From the psychobiological perspective—and more specifically according to the insights of attachment theory—the bottom line is that most people need to feel closeness and ongoing connection with another human being. That is how we're hardwired. Yes, we need people, and in particular, we tend to need one special person who can provide a sense of safety and security in the world. That in turn can reduce day-to-day stress, increase self-confidence, and make it easier to venture out and slay all the dragons in the wider environment.

Some of us regard ourselves as basically "do-it-myself" people. I'm here to make the case that, really, none of us are. And in modern adult life, another person can greatly enrich your life and help you in whatever ways you may fall short if left to go it alone. Here are a few practical examples:

- Another person can accurately guess, understand, and reflect back to you what you're going through.

- Another person can amplify your positive feelings and experiences, and assuage negative feelings and experiences.

- Another person can play with and (if needed) heal the baby within you.

- Another person can provide guidance about what to say or do when you're feeling lost or uncertain.

- Another person can step in and help when you're in trouble, emotionally or otherwise.

- Another person can boost your self-esteem when everything around you threatens to collapse.

- Another person can push you to be better than you ordinarily would be on your own.

- Another person can scratch the itch in that unreachable spot on your back (or in your soul).

People need people. You may still want to date without necessarily pair bonding. You may prefer to have lots of friends to satisfy your emotional needs, or to explore alternative forms of relationship. My purpose here is simply to guide you to improve your experience of the dating process and make better, more conscious dating decisions, based on psychobiological principles.

THE LURES AND PERILS OF ONLINE DATING

Online dating has become a very popular way to meet potential partners: according to the Pew Research Center, the percentage of Internet users who consider online dating a good way to meet people jumped from 44 percent in 2005 to 59 percent in 2013 (Desilver 2014). There are many well-known dating sites, and you can even find a specialized site for your age, ethnicity, or religion. If you believe the statistics, more than 40 million Americans have tried online dating. Among those looking for a mate, 38 percent have visited a dating site, and two-thirds of those went on a date with someone they found online. More than a third (34 percent) of Americans who have tried online dating and who are now in a committed relationship say they met their partner online (Smith and Duggan 2013).

Clearly this is a force to be reckoned with. But does it work? As a couple therapist, I've seen many couples who are in successful committed relationships with someone they met through an online dating website. However, online dating comes with some undeniable perils. People can and do lie about themselves. Some are looking for sex and not a love relationship, and they may not be up front about this. Others are simply serial daters: with the ease of online dating, people can line up several dates in a week, and you may unknowingly be just one of many. That in itself can be hurtful if it makes you feel like an easily disposable date.

Another situation in which online dating can be especially problematic is when it occurs in the context of a long-distance relationship. The physical separation creates a delay in reality testing, and couples may maintain at-a-distance relationships over months if not years. I understand that for some this is necessary due to their respective business locations. Or one partner may have a job that requires travel all over the world. If this long-distance arrangement develops later in a relationship, when partners are already committed to each other, the relationship may be able to weather the separation. However, choosing a long-distance arrangement because one or both partners find distance less threatening than closeness never bodes well for the future of a relationship.

Of course, online dating does not necessarily imply a long-distance relationship. Today a plethora of mobile apps can help people find partners within a radius of a few miles. Thus, if you are interested in online dating, you can do so without introducing the issue of distance. You can enjoy an expanded dating pool, compared with what is available to you solely through traditional avenues, and do so within your local area.

Here are some basic online dating dos and don'ts:

- Do be honest about yourself.

- Don't assume a date is being completely honest about himself or herself.

- Do your best to vet the potential date by asking questions of him or her and by getting the opinion of others you trust. (We will talk more about vetting in the next chapter—it's a process that applies to potential partners met either online or otherwise.)

- Don't decide to date someone solely on the basis of a photo or photos.

- Do meet in person sooner rather than later once you know you are interested.

- Don't launch into a virtual relationship without meeting.

- Do keep safety in mind; for example, meet in a public place and avoid disclosing personal information (such as your home address).

In general, meeting someone online (and relatively local) is not all that different from meeting someone on the street, at a party, through friends, or on a blind date. In each case, it's pretty much a roll of the dice. And in each case, it is up to you to be armed with a set of tools with which to choose and vet your potential mates. In the chapters that follow, we'll see how the various steps of the dating process play out when online dating is involved.

DISPELLING SOME LOVE RELATIONSHIP MYTHS

Before we go any further, I want to talk about some common ideas—I would call them *myths*—about love relationships. Many ideas that I believe make it harder to find a partner—or at least to have a happy experience doing so—have taken hold to varying degrees in our collective minds. If you are interested in understanding how you are wired for dating, and want to use that understanding to your best advantage, I suggest carefully reassessing each of these myths.

MYTH 1: LOVE IS ALL YOU NEED TO MAKE A RELATIONSHIP SUCCEED

Perhaps when you think about "love," you're hoping for a giddy, mushy, thunderstruck feeling, the promise of which lures you into the dating journey (and that later entices you to make promises you otherwise never would). If this is the case, I have to say no: that sort of love is *not* all you need. For starters, along with that mushy feeling, a variety of other ingredients are essential if a dating relationship is going to lead to a long-term love relationship. Above all else, you and your partner need to offer each other safety and security. You need to be able to protect each other and count on each other, and find a way of being together that is mutually beneficial, fair, just, and sensitive. This is not the heart-racing thrill of love, but it is the stuff of lasting relationship. Love matters, of course, but it has to be demythologized before you can venture to live according to any maxim that uses the word.

One way you can bust any myths you have about love is to carefully consider what love means to you. Earlier, I asked you to picture your ideal partner. In the following exercise I'm suggesting you get a clear picture of something more abstract: love itself.

EXERCISE: LOVE DEFINED

What is love, really? Here are some steps to help you clarify your views.

1. Collect some quotes, from books or from the Web, about love. See what the great ones have to say about

love. And if you wish, you can add your own truisms to the list. Here are some classics:

- Love is a smoke made with the fume of sighs. —Shakespeare

- Love is a canvas furnished by nature and embroidered by imagination. —Voltaire

- Love is space and time measured by the heart. —Proust

- Love is a willingness to sacrifice. —Michael Novak

- Love is like a virus. It can happen to anybody at any time. —Maya Angelou

- Love is metaphysical gravity. —R. Buckminster Fuller

- Love is a cloud that scatters pearls. —Rumi

- Love is the greatest refreshment in life. —Picasso

- Love is a growing up. —James Baldwin

2. Brainstorm words or phrases that define "love" for you. At this stage, it's okay if your definition is abstract or poetic. In fact, if you feel moved to do so, see if your own words form a poem.

3. Now take your definition of love and concretize it. You may find it helpful to complete the following sentence:

"For my ideal relationship to work, the love between my partner and I must be/include _____."

At some point down the line, if a dating relationship progresses far enough, love will enter the picture. One or the other of you will be the first to utter the word. When that happens, you may wish to revisit your definition of love.

MYTH 2: YOU HAVE TO LOVE YOURSELF BEFORE YOU CAN LOVE SOMEONE ELSE

If this were true, a baby would have to love itself before it was able to love its mother. But that's not what happens: a baby learns to love from being loved. For a baby, there is no loving without feeling loved, or vice versa. The two work in tandem, inseparable. In fact, the baby experiences being loved and loving before it has any concept of what love is. Moreover, self-love becomes meaningful only after a child experiences a sense of separate self. That typically occurs after a child's first birthday. (Pediatrician T. Berry Brazelton [1992] and others have researched and written at length on this topic.) Suffice it to say that, in our earliest stages of development, love is like a vast ocean whose waves do not distinguish between self and other.

The myth of self-love being primary implies that, as an adult, you should stop right now, go somewhere, and learn to love yourself before you embark on the dating journey. It supposes that you can generate self-love by taking a class, reading a book, or meditating in a cave. But you can't. You learn to love by engaging with others, period. It can't be done alone.

Some people turn to this myth because they feel they cease to exist as a whole person while in a relationship, or even while dating. This feels so threatening that they decide the only solution is to opt out, at least for now, and avoid the risk until they have somehow become strong, self-loving, and ready. I believe the opposite is true—that if you were hurt in a relationship, then *only* a relationship can heal you. Couple therapist Harville Hendrix (2007) puts it more explicitly: "In order to heal the wounds of the past, you need to receive love from a person whom your unconscious mind has merged with your childhood caregivers." You might say you're not ready for that. Okay. In that case, perhaps therapy would be a good place to start. Or just hanging out with friends for a while (friendship is a vital form of relationship, and can be very healing). Or having the experience of living alone, for once. Or even just sticking to the company of pets or plants, or getting involved with an interesting hobby. You may need to seek solace in situations that feel less emotionally risky, at least temporarily. But if you want to find a special someone, eventually you will have to jump into the dating world. You might not feel completely ready for a love relationship, but see if you are ready to *learn* to love—both yourself and another.

MYTH 3: YOU HAVE TO LEARN TO TAKE CARE OF YOURSELF BEFORE YOU CAN START DATING

Myth #3 is related to Myth #2. People who espouse this myth may be fearful of becoming too dependent on another person. They may lack confidence in their ability to leave a romantic relationship when and if necessary. Fear of abandonment eclipses all other matters, including their own happiness in a relationship.

Again, think of an infant. A baby is dependent upon its mother for everything. But that is what we expect for a baby—the mother-infant relationship is not a relationship of equals. The notion that you have to take care of yourself first risks presupposing that you and your partner couldn't share the kind of mutuality in which you both agree to take care of each other; or it suggests that you do not trust and welcome that mutual responsibility.

One way to grasp the impact of this myth is to put the shoe on the other foot. Imagine a potential partner saying, "I need to take care of myself first." Now check your gut. How does that make you feel? Disregarded? Unimportant? Maybe even unloved? Whatever it is, I bet it's not great. Even if it feels good (or safe, or strong) for you to say it, it probably doesn't feel so good for you to hear it. That's because the statement itself is threatening to your relationship. It says, in essence, "I'm on my own, and you're on your own." In other words, it means both "Don't look to me to keep you secure" and "I don't trust you to care for me."

These days, this kind of pro-self view is quite prevalent. Many people value the notion of putting themselves first, and our culture supports that stance. The idea of being pro-relationship, and of being in each other's care rather than each on your own, may seem like anathema to you. It may go against everything your experience has taught you to be true. No problem: you don't have to throw out a belief because I call it into question. At this point, my suggestion is simply that you keep an open mind as you go through this book.

MYTH 4: YOU SHOULDN'T RELY ON ONLY ONE PERSON FOR YOUR WELL-BEING

In other words, no potential partner will be able to satisfy all your wants and needs; Myth #4 is in that sense a permutation of Myth #3. And in fact, there is some actual truth to this truism. It is never healthy to restrict your relational needs to one person, to the exclusion of all others. Couples who isolate themselves in this way, without a social network, are at risk of falling into what is known as a folie à deux. We will look at this in chapter 7.

But this is not what I mean when I cite this idea as a "myth." I do so because many people use it to define a pro-self rather than pro-relationship stance, and to avoid creating greater closeness with a partner. For example: "Please don't depend on *me* so much." Or "I can't depend on anyone, so I won't depend on you because you're bound to let me down." Or "No one person will satisfy me...so I'll have many."

You can and should be able to depend on just one person— namely, the person you choose—as long as that person is dependable and you, too, are dependable. You both can depend on each other. To use a military metaphor, the question to answer is, "Are the two of you in a foxhole together, or are you in separate foxholes?" If you are in a foxhole together, you not only can rely on each other, but you have to do so for your very survival. Believing that relying on one person is a bad idea prevents you from dating someone with whom you will be able to create a relationship that offers the safety and security you need.

MYTH 5: I NEED TO FIND MY SOUL MATE

This myth is "There is only one soul mate for me"—meaning, "There is one person out there for me."

So, tell me, how many soul mates do you think are out there for you? One? Two? A dozen? Hundreds? I bet you're not thinking in terms of hundreds. Just one, right? But if there really is just one, and you're already struggling in the dating world, I must say the numbers definitely are not in your favor. Even if there are ten people out there for you, you're still up a creek. What are the odds you will be able to find one of those ten among the other seven billion? You'd have a much easier time finding the proverbial needle in a haystack.

You might feel that you are a romantic and that destiny dictates you find the one person who can make you happy. I'm afraid that sort of happiness will elude you; again, it's a numbers problem. Moreover, you change as you age. What you think will make you happy now may not be what you want or need five, ten, or twenty years from now. Some people pattern their ideal partner after their continuously changing feeling state. A real person could never compete with that. For both these reasons—the numbers, and the changeability of human nature—rather than holding out for the one and only perfect person out there, I suggest you think in terms of many possible people, any of whom could love and accept you as you change and grow throughout your lifetime.

As we will see in the next chapter, your brain picks partners based on familiarity, not on the possibility you shared a previous life or anything of that nature. In truth, there are many, many, many potential soul mates for you out there. And all are unique. Every primary love relationship is unique, like a fingerprint, and cannot be duplicated. Any two partners create between them a third entity, which is their relationship. That relationship has a personality unto itself, which is one reason we mourn its end so strongly: when it is over, it will never exist again. The next relationship will be different because the individuals involved will be different.

Could many potential partners be your soul mates? Only you can answer that question—or, more accurately, your brain can. Your subconscious mind will consider anyone with whom you feel familiarity and recognition a good candidate—at least in the short run. Then it will be up to you to go through the dating process and decide if he or she is a viable long-term prospect. As far as soul mate status, I leave it to you and your eventual partner to decide whether you want to give each other that title.

MYTH 6: DATING IS FOR THE YOUNG— I'M TOO OLD

No ambiguity about this one: it's not true at all. Young people have less life experience than their elders do, and thus tend to be less knowledgeable about themselves. This makes the dating process more simplistic, but also more error prone. Generally speaking, as we age, we become more fluid and flexible with ourselves and others. We are more aware of our mortality and of the fact that we can't do everything. We have a better sense of what we do and don't like, and our priorities are different—perhaps relationships and family have become more important than career. When it comes time to meet a new partner, we can present ourselves in a more realistic fashion.

Of course, some dating disadvantages can also come with age. For example, if you have loved and lost, you may be reluctant to try again. And even though you have the natural confidence that comes with age, it may elude you in the dating arena. One reason some older people lose confidence when it comes to dating is that they have age-related image concerns. At first glance, this may appear especially true for women, but it cuts both ways. We will discuss this issue more later, but for now it's sufficient to say that the natural aging process is unrelated to the ability to form a loving, accepting, secure-functioning relationship.

This book is written for people of all ages. If you are young and inexperienced, I would like to save you some years of trouble. If you are older, I want you to understand that age is not an obstacle and that you are in a good position to find a partner worthy of your efforts.

FINAL THOUGHTS

Relationships can take any form. But if you want to be in a committed relationship, there are some basic dos and don'ts from a psychobiological perspective. Ongoing work in this field means we now know, on a physiological and psychological level, which factors and conditions are likely to lead to a successful relationship and which are likely to lead to a relationship's doom. We can prescribe guidelines and principles to follow if you want to find and stay with a partner. This might not seem so important during the infatuation phase, but by the time you approach the commitment phase, it becomes crucial. So, as you gear up for dating, it's not too soon to start thinking along the lines described in this book.

As we go, I will share more research with you, as well as skills and principles I suggest you learn. Knowing how your brain is wired will go a long way toward helping you understand how you choose and respond to a partner. Some of the inexplicable behaviors you have witnessed in yourself and others will suddenly become clear. In addition, a certain amount of rewiring may be necessary to ensure that the dating process goes as smoothly as possible. That's what I mean by *learning*. You will discover how to identify and correct any ways you currently approach dating that may be counterproductive— and you will begin to practice new skills and perspectives, rewiring your brain for dating, and for relationship.

In the next chapter, we look more closely at how neurobiology influences you during the earliest steps in the dating process, as you begin to date and to figure out whether a partner is potentially the right one for you. Ready?

CHAPTER 2

Seeing Clearly Through the Fog of Infatuation

With this chapter, we begin the dating journey in earnest. Here we focus on the initial phase of that process; specifically, the first few dates. This is when critical decisions are made that will shape your future dating and relationship prospects. Foremost among these are decisions about who attracts you and whether you are going to go on that next date. You might not think you actually make decisions about this, but trust me, you do. I'm going to show you—literally, from the inside out—how this process takes place.

This chapter draws heavily on the neuroscience component of the psychobiological approach. I won't get overly technical, but I do want you to understand the role that *neurochemicals* of love play in your recognition of a potential partner, as well as in sexual attraction. Neurochemicals, including hormones and neurotransmitters, are the substances that serve as the functional elements of your nervous system. It is these neurochemicals and the pathways through which they travel that determine how you are "wired." Visual perception and familiarity are two neurobiological functions that also matter when it comes to choosing a partner, and we'll look at how they play a role in the initial stages of dating. We'll also discuss the importance of vetting, or screening, your future partners, and you will have an opportunity to assess and sharpen your skills in this area.

A Walk in the Park

Let's start by meeting Milo, a twenty-five-year-old actor. One morning he sees a young woman walking her Yorkie in his neighborhood park. The attraction is immediate, so he strikes up a conversation. Milo and the woman, Kathy, instantly become so enchanted with each other that they end up spending the rest of the day together. They walk, they talk, they eat. At sunset, they settle onto a stone bench in the corner of the park and begin passionately kissing.

Milo can't get enough of Kathy, and she seems to feel the same. Everything seems right about her: her face, her body, the way she smells, the way she tastes, the way she kisses. He experiences an epiphany: he'd been looking for the perfect partner for years, and now here she is!

Around midnight, the pair begin the long walk back to Kathy's apartment, holding hands and stopping to kiss at every street corner. At the apartment, the kissing escalates into groping and fondling. To Milo, this isn't mere horniness. He is convinced they are falling in love. As the Yorkie curls up by the bed, their fondling leads to undressing, then to more intimate fondling. Finally, just as the sun is coming up, Kathy draws the line at intercourse.

"It's too soon," she whispers. "You understand?"

Reluctantly, Milo agrees. He would never have let things even get that far if he weren't absolutely convinced that he just met his soul mate. And so begins their slow farewell: long kisses while getting dressed, long kisses at the door, and one last kiss after he has stepped into the hallway.

Milo is walking on air despite the fact that he's had no sleep. He lies down for two hours, then showers, puts on his workout clothes, and heads for the gym. He can't get Kathy out of his mind. He has a rehearsal that afternoon, but as soon as it is over, he plans to stop by her place. He can hardly wait to see her again.

Imagine Milo's surprise as he walks into the gym and spots Kathy working out on a stationary bicycle. Clearly this is destiny! Here she is, working out at the gym he's been coming to for years. He rushes over. As he approaches, however, he realizes she is engaged in conversation with the young man on the bike next to hers. The man says something, and she throws back her head and laughs, then leans over and…kisses him. Milo freezes. "Did she see me?" he asks himself.

Before he can steal away, Kathy looks up. "Hi," she says quickly, in the manner of a stranger.

Milo ekes out a faint "hi" in return.

Kathy returns her smiling gaze to the man at her side. It is as if she doesn't even recognize Milo. But how can that be? They spent a full day together, much of it lip locked, and it has only been a few hours since they separated. Yes, he has put on his workout clothes, but that shouldn't make him unrecognizable.

"Excuse me," he blurts out. "Don't you recognize me?"

Rather blithely, because she apparently doesn't want the biker beside her to get any wrong ideas, Kathy answers, "Should I?"

Feeling dismissed, confused, and humiliated, Milo walks away. He and Kathy never speak again, so he never finds out why she didn't recognize him or why she pretended not to.

So what went wrong?

You might say, "They moved too fast." Or "They didn't get to know each other well enough." Or "They were looking for different things." You might lay blame more on one or the other: "He was naïve, too focused on chemistry." Or "She was a total [fill in the blank]; he got duped."

All these responses have varying degrees of relevance. However, I would say none gets to the core of the issue. When considering what went wrong, I think two things are most helpful: (a) understanding what really caused Milo to act as he did, and (b) identifying what he didn't do that he should have done and vice versa. In addition, we can consider why Kathy acted as she did, and how she could have acted differently. The sections that follow address all these issues and help you gear up for your own dating adventures.

Love's Neurochemical Cocktail

You won't be able to understand what was happening to Milo—or to yourself as you go about picking a partner—unless you are familiar with some of the basic principles of neurochemistry. When Milo saw Kathy walking her dog, he thought destiny was at work. In reality, chemical substances within him were running the whole show. At the first glimpse of Kathy, a veritable cocktail of neurochemicals began brewing in his brain and body, creating a fog of infatuation that made him unable to think clearly or act reasonably. Let's look at the mechanics of this process in detail.

During your first encounter with a potential partner, you quickly become saturated with a mix of hormones and neurochemicals that make you feel simultaneously excited, attentive, interested, and even slightly anxious. These aren't chemicals that come out of nowhere; they exist within you all along; however, their levels rise or fall in response to circumstances. In this case, an attractive man or woman is the catalyst for the change. This isn't something you can consciously control.

The neurochemical response occurs automatically, triggered by parts of the brain I call the *primitives* because they are oriented primarily toward basic survival and they function without conscious control. Here's where things get a bit technical. But I want to make sure you have the facts. So please bear with me.

The basic love cocktail includes the following primary chemicals: testosterone, estrogen, dopamine, noradrenaline, serotonin, oxytocin, and vasopressin. These, along with other ingredients, exert varying effects at different times, but generally speaking, they are nature's way of intoxicating you so you go for it when you meet someone appealing. Your primitives aren't particularly interested in establishing happy long-term relationships. (Sorry.)

Biological anthropologist Helen Fisher and her colleagues have done extensive research on the role of neurochemicals during the dating process. In a seminal article published in 2002, they proposed that this process involves three different neural systems—that is, three types of wiring: *lust, attraction,* and *attachment.* These systems are not necessarily sequential or mutually exclusive. For this discussion of what happens as you meet a potential partner and begin to date, we are most interested in the systems of lust and attraction—in other words, the ingredients of infatuation. Attachment comes later.

With respect to lust, or the physical aspect of initial attraction, you are probably familiar with the two main hormones that come into play: testosterone and estrogen. You may associate testosterone with men and estrogen with women. This is partially correct; in fact, testosterone exists within both men and women. And it gets even more complicated and counterintuitive. Scientists have found that testosterone levels drop in men when they are falling in love, and rise in women when they are falling in love. Notably, however, these changes are temporary; within a year or two, testosterone returns to the levels found in men and women who are not in love.

With respect to attraction, neurochemicals that play major roles include dopamine, noradrenaline, and serotonin. When Fisher and her team (2010) studied the brain scans of individuals who were looking at photos of their loved ones, they found that certain parts of their brain—the caudate nucleus and ventral tegmental area, both primitives—lit up. When they looked at photos with neutral emotion content, these areas did not get activated. What is significant about this finding is that these are the most dopamine-rich areas of the brain. They could be called your brain's pleasure center. *Dopamine* levels rise when you are feeling good—for example, because you just spotted a potential love interest. Dopamine is responsible for the rush of pleasure and energy and desire you feel on a first date. It can make you care less about food or sleep or other aspects of your normal life, and become preoccupied with the new relationship. The more dopamine is activated within you, the more you want it. In fact, dopamine plays a huge role in the brain's reward circuit. For this reason, Fisher likens the excitement phase of love—or infatuation—to a chemical addiction.

Noradrenaline is the neurochemical that triggers a rush of adrenaline. This is why your hands sweat and your heart races when you go on that first date. You are simultaneously energized and anxious, and you are very attentive. Of course, this is not sustainable. The more time you spend in the company of your new love object, the less noradrenaline is a factor; thus you feel less scared, but you also become less attentive.

Perhaps the most interesting neurochemical in the mix is *serotonin*. Exactly how serotonin works in the body is not fully understood, but the many functions it appears to affect are quite diverse, including mood and social behavior, sleep, memory, appetite, and sexual attraction. For example, some popular psychiatric drugs, known as *selective serotonin reuptake inhibitors*, or SSRIs, increase levels of serotonin. Many people with depression or obsessive-compulsive disorder (OCD) have low levels of serotonin, and taking SSRIs can reduce their symptoms. So what does this have to do with your attraction to the attractive gal or guy who just crossed your path? Well, it turns out that attraction also lowers serotonin. In one classic study, published in 1999, Donatella Marazziti and her colleagues in Italy measured serotonin levels in three groups: individuals who said they had fallen in love; individuals suffering from OCD; and "normal" individuals who were neither in love nor obsessive. Serotonin levels were about 40 percent lower in both of the first groups than in the so-called normal group. This certainly gives new meaning to the expression "crazy in love"! But again, as in the case of other neurochemicals and hormones, these changes do not last, and serotonin levels return to normal a year or two after you fall in love.

Before we leave the topic of serotonin, there is one additional fact worth mentioning. Individuals who take SSRIs—and their potential partners—may be at a disadvantage when dating. Whereas low levels of serotonin are one of nature's way of getting new lovers to obsess about one another, SSRIs remove that incentive. Suppose I am on an SSRI and I meet you at a party. With the help of dopamine and noradrenaline and the rest of the neurochemical cocktail, I may get excited in the moment. But the next day, I may think, *Meh.* Too bad if you're obsessing about me, because I'm not obsessing about you. Someone who is taking an SSRI can go on dates and live off the excitatory chemicals in his or her brain and body without ever settling on any partner. I'm not suggesting you screen your dates to see if they're on antidepressants, or that you go off one yourself. But this is an issue that can come into play in some cases.

I also mentioned oxytocin and vasopressin. These two are more important after you have begun to form a bond with a potential partner. But let's come back to Milo and Kathy for a moment. All the knowledge about Kathy that Milo acquired during their day together was a creation of his chemically driven imagination; a mix of dopamine and other neurochemicals clouded his reasoning and gave him a false green light when it came to Kathy. This phenomenon, captured by the old adage "love is blind," is one of nature's powerful illusions. As it turned out, Kathy was not as fully blinded as Milo was, and she was able to hold the line at intercourse.

What could Milo have done to avoid setting himself up for the pain he felt when Kathy dismissed him? Simply becoming aware of the powerful influence of the neurochemical cocktail would be a good starting point for Milo—and in all likelihood for Kathy, as well. This can be difficult to do in the heat of the moment, but with practice, you can learn to step back and remind yourself that chemical forces are affecting your feelings and emotions. You don't have to remember the names of the various neurochemicals, and I'm certainly not suggesting you go for a brain scan after your date! But you can learn to recognize some of the effects of these neurochemicals. Notice when your hands get sweaty and your heart races when you are around a potential partner. Notice changes in your appetite and sleep patterns. Let these kinds of signs serve as clues that you may be vulnerable to the fog of infatuation. I'm not saying you should stop dating because you experience the effects of these powerful chemicals. You can benefit simply from being aware of them—an awareness that would have helped Milo stay grounded.

However, perhaps the most important thing Milo should have done was begin the process of vetting his partner before he spent a significant amount of time with her. *Vetting* (in any context) means thoroughly investigating someone before you proceed further with that person. Candidates for a job, for example, go through a series of vetting interviews and background checks. If the job requires secrecy or confidentiality, the vetting is especially stringent. In the context of dating, we can break the vetting process into three phases: (1) the initial screening you do yourself; (2) the deeper vetting others can do for you; and (3) the ongoing assessment—which I like to call sherlocking (see chapter 4)—that you do with a potential partner who has passed the initial screening. In this case, if Milo had been able to remind himself that he had learned very little about Kathy's life and habits during their few hours together, he might have been able to spare himself the pain and humiliation that came from their meeting the next day. Instead, he let himself believe he was in love, that she was The One, and that it was mutual. The important point here is that it takes time and effort to know a person, and that it's never too soon to start investigating a potential partner.

Before I talk more about the vetting process, though, I need to mention two other neurological functions that influence how we choose a partner: the visual system, and the brain's emphasis on familiarity.

VISION MATTERS

Primitives and neurochemicals are not the sole influences when we meet a potential partner. How we see him or her also has an effect. By "see," I mean literally how our eyes take in that person. Neuroscientists recognize two primary ways in which the eyes operate. The first is the *far visual* system (or *dorsal visual stream*), which is more closely tied with the primitives. This system does not have much capacity for detail. The second is the *near visual* system (or *ventral visual stream*). This system, which is more detailed and precise, works more closely with what I call the *ambassadors*. In contrast with the primitives, the ambassadors are the more evolved, social part of the brain. Rather than acting on memory and reflex, as the primitives do, they make more nuanced judgments.

When you see someone at a distance, your far visual system is good at catching broad movements of the body and basic physical characteristics. This comes in handy for detecting danger. For example, if you see a stranger moving toward you in a menacing manner, your internal alarm may go off: "Who's that?" "Am I in harm's way?" By recognizing dangerous movements in this way, you have a few seconds of warning to save yourself.

As it turns out, this same system is also good at picking up signals of attraction. It is especially good for lust. For instance, when Kathy was walking her dog, Milo's far visual system picked up the way she swung her hips, her tight clothing, her long hair. This limited information incited his primitives to recognize her as sexy. It didn't matter that her face was still not clear, not to mention that he couldn't know anything about her ideas, interests, or personality.

As you move closer to a person, your near visual system and ambassadors swing into action. They are equipped to take in information from every muscle in the other person's face, as well as his or her eyes, including the pupils. Moreover, not only can you see the other person close up, but he or she can see you. You are both at a similar advantage—or disadvantage—in this regard. You are literally looking into each other's nervous systems—live. And if you have a few drinks—Milo didn't, but it is common practice in many dating situations—the face will lose some of its natural asymmetry and appear even more pleasing than it will in the light of day.

Now, you might say, "Well, that doesn't explain why Milo acted as he did because he had opportunities to use both his primitives and his ambassadors during their day together." Of course he did. But let's face it, Milo was high on nature's cocktail, and primarily under the sway of information obtained through his primitives. He and Kathy would have needed much more close-up, face-to-face contact to really get to know one another. Only such ongoing, sustained close contact can override the powerful but misleading impressions gained from a distance.

You can get a sense of how your visual systems work next time you are at a park or a mall or a bus stop—any place that's good for people watching. Do a little experiment. Compare the information you take in from someone at a distance with what you can see when people are up close. If you get a better sense of how your visual systems work, you can apply this knowledge as you go about picking partners—and even friends. You can avoid acting upon sketchy information you pick up from a distance. Instead, place your trust in your near visual system.

FAMILIARITY MATTERS

We tend to be attracted most readily to those we find familiar. By familiar, however, I don't necessarily mean *pleasantly* familiar. Consider this: Milo had a mad crush on a dark-haired girl in his class in junior high. She even had a little dog, which she would walk around with after school with her friends. She flirted with Milo often, but his heart was broken when he invited her to his birthday party and she did not show up. Milo would tell you Kathy didn't remind him of that girl because Kathy is blonde and that girl had dark hair. He did not notice what was actually familiar to him: the profound feelings of hurt and rejection.

Now, you might question how Milo could possibly have known Kathy would let him down. The point is that he wouldn't necessarily have known. This is where the automatic brain comes in. Your primitives are expert at picking people they see as familiar, even if they have relatively few cues to go on. They are primed to see aspects of yourself, or of important people from your past, reflected in someone you meet. This makes that person seem attractive in a way that could last beyond a week, a month, or a year.

You may be surprised to learn that romantic partners are more alike than not. If you say no, you're probably thinking that you had a long-term relationship with at least one partner who was the exact opposite of you or your family. While on some level you appeared to be opposites, I would wager that on a deeper, more unconscious level, aspects of that person were familiar (or familial) to you. Keep in mind that "familiar" does not necessarily mean everything is positive. Feelings of hurt and neglect can be as familiar as feelings of love and affection. This is why, for example, someone with an alcoholic father may be attracted to a potential partner who is an alcoholic. Or why someone would continue to date a person even after being repeatedly abused in that relationship.

Harry Reis (2011) and others who have studied the ways in which familiarity promotes attraction define *familiarity* as the amount of prior exposure to another person. In other words, we like, or are attracted to, something just because we have been around it. We feel safe with it, and we feel less safe with what is unfamiliar. Moreover, as we get to know someone, and that person becomes more familiar, we are more predisposed to like him or her. This is known as the *mere exposure effect*. In a classic study (done long before the days of the Internet), Richard Moreland and Robert Zajonc (1982) showed one group a photo of the same man for four weeks, and showed another group photos of a different man each week. Those who saw the same photo rated the man as more similar to themselves and more attractive, while the group who saw different photos rated them as less similar to themselves and less attractive.

None of this, by the way, is meant to imply that attraction between people of different races or ethnicities is in any way unnatural. The familiarity I am speaking about is more than skin deep. I should also mention that your brain prefers at least some strangerness with the familiarity. No one wants to partner with his or her clone, or clan, for that matter. We want someone who offers a mix of safety and security (familiarity) and novelty and excitement (unfamiliarity).

What does it mean for your own dating journey? First and foremost, it is something to be aware of. See if you can notice what feels familiar and what does not, and try to understand why. In later chapters, we will look more closely at how you can distinguish between familiar behaviors that can be used to build a lasting relationship and familiar behaviors that are best to avoid.

VETTING YOUR PARTNER

When Cinda fell in love with Bob, she didn't bother taking him to meet her parents because she already knew they would disapprove. Bob was twenty years her senior, plus she figured he was too debonair for her parents' liking. She did introduce Bob to her friends, though. Her girlfriends loved him. They were impressed with the gifts he gave her and went wild over photos of his summer beach home. Cinda never asked her girlfriends' boyfriends what they thought of Bob until it was too late.

Cinda dated Bob for one year and was engaged to him for one month before she found out who he really was. To say he cheated on her would be an understatement. He was unfaithful from the beginning right up to the day she caught him, which was (to her credit) the end of their relationship.

In the aftermath, her male friends shared their impressions of Bob: "A real scumbag. I could tell the first time I met him." "The guy was a player. He tried to hit on my girlfriend." "You were so into him, I didn't want to mention what he said when you were out of the room."

What if she had married him? What if they'd had children? The outcome could have been much worse. Moreover, in this case, understanding the role of neurochemicals and the influence of visual systems and familiarity is insufficient to answer to the question "What went wrong?" Understanding the importance of familiarity might have helped Cinda realize she and Bob did not have enough in common for a good partnership. Still, even that would not have alerted her that he was likely to cheat on her.

What went wrong here is simple: partners need to socially vet each other with both male and female friends and family before they get serious about dating each other. Cinda failed to do this.

In chapter 1, I asked you to list the characteristics you want in a partner. This is a valuable exercise (which, by the way, was done by the ambassadors in your brain) because it is good to be clear about what you want. At the same time, I think our discussion so far illustrates that your primitives don't care much about your list. The fact that they select partners based on biology, facial symmetry, smell, taste, touch, and other factors outside your control has been widely researched and documented over the past several decades. If you use your ambassador-created list to select a date, that person may be a perfect match on paper, but your primitives may not be on board. And if your body says no, then it's a no. Conversely, you could say to heck with it all and go out with someone who has none of the items on your list, and your primitives won't stop you. Not the right one for you for the long run? Too bad.

Some people say, "I have a bad picker. I keep picking the wrong people!" But I would say that your picker is very good at finding the right people for you—at least from its perspective. Your picker is not your problem. In fact, there really is no such thing as a bad picker. Your problem is very likely that you don't have a social network that helps you vet your partner for you. In other words, you are picking a partner based on the whims and dictates of your primitives, without sufficient ambassador input.

YOUR SOCIAL NETWORK

Ideally, you could rely on your own ambassadors to vet a new partner. And to a certain extent, you have to learn to do that. You have to perform an initial screening, then follow that up with a longer process of inquiry, drawing on your social network, as you get to know your potential partner. Milo is a prime example. He needed to do some quick screening of his own with Kathy, even before he would have had an opportunity to bring in other people. He needed to ask some appropriate questions before his hormones took his mind for a ride. In the next chapter, we will examine specific ways to check your partner out using your own mindful awareness and asking the right kinds of questions.

Nevertheless, using your own ambassadors has its limits. If your primitives and ambassadors disagree, who's going to mediate? For this reason, you also want to call in outside consultation with friends and family. Call upon *their* ambassadors. In fact, if there's something to be said for arranged marriages, especially ones arranged by kin, it is that the family likely will take the time to vet a partner based on familiarity, recognition, and familial similarity rather than letting first impressions rule their choice.

Let me share how my wife, Tracey, and I vetted each other. To start with, we were familiar because we went to the same secondary school. Back then, I was a shy musician, and Tracey was an outgoing athlete. Because we came from two different groups, we did not hang together. Fast-forward several decades. After my divorce, I found Tracey's name on our school's alumni website. I emailed her, thinking she was probably married. As it turned out, she was also divorced and had a daughter, Joanna, who was ten at the time.

Despite our familiarity, Tracey and I are different from each other in some obvious ways. Our initial screening of each other uncovered these differences, as well as important similarities. For example, Tracey is Christian and mainly of German heritage, while I am Jewish and of Russian origin. However, Tracey has many traits that remind me of my own family, while I was raised (in part) by a Catholic woman. We both grew up in affluent families and share similar values and a sense of moral justice and fairness. We have very similar sensibilities when it comes to friendships and are both wildly social animals.

Neither Tracey nor I had vetted our previous partners with our friends or families, at least not extensively. When we began dating seriously, we knew we didn't want to repeat our earlier relationship failures. So we made sure to vet each other as fully and carefully as possible by parading each other around to our families and friends.

Tracey's parents died when she was in her early twenties, so we spent a lot of time with her sisters and their husbands, including going on vacations with the extended family. We had dinners with her friends and their husbands, and even went on some small trips with them. I think our families, in general, found us to be as different from them as we were familiar. Over a year's time, we gained the blessings of all of our friends and family. People commented on how happy we were. We looked younger and healthier, they said. Both of our careers began to flourish. Our relationships with others improved. Interestingly, we both agree that if we had tried to get together a few years earlier, we might not have found ourselves so well suited.

One note of caution: This isn't to say that vetting your partner with all your peeps is foolproof. It isn't. We've all heard stories of partners who were well liked and approved of by family and friends, but turned out to be psychopaths. However, this isn't so common that you need to worry about it.

EXERCISE: THUMBS UP OR DOWN

This is more than a simple exercise you can do while you read this book. It is a process to go through with anyone you are currently dating (if you haven't already) or with the next potential partner you think you might get serious about. I want you to thoroughly vet this person before you go any further.

1. Select at least three vetters for your date: (1) a family member; (2) a member of the same gender; and (3) a member of the opposite gender. I say a minimum of three, but that doesn't preclude more. In fact, the more the merrier. Pick people whom know you well and will tell it to you straight. It also helps if they are relationship "vets"—meaning that in addition to being vetters, they are veterans of relationships themselves.

    If your family doesn't live nearby, try Skype. If you don't have family, substitute someone who feels most like family to you. If you think, like Cinda, that your family will object, well, then you have your answer right there.

    If you are a same-sex couple (or couple-to-be) and wonder about the need for opinions from the opposite gender, I say why not? If you prefer, you can get all your opinions from friends of the same gender. The point is to get as many viewpoints as possible.

2. Call the vetters and arrange a place and time to meet. You don't have to tell them you consider them vetters.

And you don't have to explain this to your date, either. In other words, getting together with your date and a friend or family member can be a natural event at this stage of your relationship, so treat it as such.

You could meet all the vetters at one time, but that often works only if they are all family. The event doesn't have to be anything too formal; you could have dinner or coffee or go for a walk. Make sure there is plenty of time for interaction; in other words, don't introduce your date to your vetters at the movies.

3. After the introduction has occurred, arrange a time to speak with your vetters. This is best done individually, and at this point, make it clear that you are seeking their opinions. Ask each the following:

    •   What did you like about my date?

    •   What did you like about me when I was with my date? Was I myself? Was I different? (If so, how?)

    •   How did you think my date treated me? (Please give specific examples.)

    •   Did we look comfortable and relaxed with each other? (Please give specific examples.)

    •   Can you picture me with this person long term? (If so, why? If not, why?)

    •   Did you notice any red flags? (Please be specific.)

    •   If you had to vote now, would it be thumbs up or thumbs down?

As you are holding this conversation, do your best simply to listen and not be defensive, either with respect to the feedback about your date or with respect to your own choices. Remember, the purpose is to get honest input from people you trust. You are not obligated to follow their advice. But I highly recommend you give it serious consideration, even if it ends up not being what you wanted to hear.

It is quite possible you will get contradictory recommendations from your three vetters. In this case, you can use the information in the following ways. First, notice where the majority opinion is, and see if that resonates with you. Second, return to your vetters and ask follow-up questions to clarify how they came to their conclusions. Ask for additional specific examples. Finally, err on the side of caution, especially in the case of potential red flags. Red flags your vetters might notice include your date being inappropriately flirtatious, trying too hard to appear a certain way, putting you down behind your back, or any kind of inconsiderate or obnoxious behavior.

FINAL THOUGHTS

At its best, dating feels like a natural process, something you can do without too much thought or effort. Probably you'd prefer your dating experience go smoothly, like playing flawlessly at a concert or dancing at a recital or giving a stellar performance in front of an audience. I'm sure you don't want to make mistakes or bumble about. But you will. Dating is a learning process—more like learning to play harmony than giving a virtuoso performance. Besides, when it comes to relationships, our neurobiology ensures that we mess up. Our primitives will do something that our ambassadors can't correct, or at least not instantaneously. And the same will be true for your partner.

What I am counting on is that you will benefit simply from becoming more aware of the neurobiological forces at work within you. The fog of infatuation can seem quite thick at times, but you don't need to get lost in it. At the very least, you can blame those flagrant neurochemicals for any missteps; at best, you have gained a deeper understanding of your own makeup. Don't underestimate the power of knowing yourself. You may be tempted to dismiss my advice in this chapter because it does not sound like a practical technique. But I believe it is the foundation of your success in the dating world. If you don't make the effort both to know yourself and to understand how you are wired for dating, no technique—and there are books full of them—will be able to save you from dating failure.

In addition to the ability to see more clearly through the fog of infatuation, drawing on your social network to vet a potential partner can greatly improve the odds of success. Considering the propensity of our hormones to drive us to do crazy things, having friends and family weigh in and provide some perspective is a must. This will give you a solid start on good dating practice—and there's a lot more work to do. In the next chapter, we're going to look at what you can do to push through any jitters you are feeling and put your best foot forward on a date.

CHAPTER 3

Dealing with the Dating Jitters

Which of the following do you associate with the experience of a first date? Stomach butterflies. Jitters. Clammy hands. Wet armpits. Loss of appetite. Nail biting. Awkward silences. Panic. Racing pulse. Embarrassment. Lightheadedness or dizziness. Shaky knees. Being tongue-tied. Uncertainty...

Or perhaps none of these apply to you. Instead you would describe yourself as generally calm, cool, collected, confident, articulate, smiling, relaxed. If you can honestly say the latter, great. More power to you. You can skip this chapter. But if your description falls anywhere short of that, we have some things to discuss.

In this chapter, we look at how you can put your best foot forward in a new dating relationship. You may be familiar with the typical advice for first dates: dress appropriately; don't be late; keep the date relatively short; above all, don't start blabbing about your ex; and so on. Such advice is well taken. But let's take it a step further. In the last chapter, I drew on neuroscience principles to explain how your nervous system responds to a potential partner. Here I'll expand on this topic so you can learn to actually work with your own nervous system to improve your dating experience.

We'll start by looking at how the nervous system operates under stress during a dating situation, and at the role of performance anxiety.

Once you are aware of how your nervous system is reacting, even if it is reacting automatically, you are in a better position to counteract it. The main psychobiological technique I suggest is becoming mindfully aware of the workings of your own nervous system. This approach may take some getting used to, but it comes with solid scientific backing, and I think you will find it both fun and transformative.

PERFORMANCE ANXIETY ON A DATE

If you're like most people, you feel—and probably appear to others—differently on a date than you do at many other times and in many other situations in your life. You might think this is a condition unique to you, or that it is something you should have figured out how to overcome by now. Not so. In fact, what many of us go through on the dating journey can be likened to the kind of stress faced by Olympic athletes and stage performers, such as dancers, comedians, actors, and the like. The common assumption in dating is that a winning performance is required to stay in the game. And this can be highly anxiety provoking. Athletes and performers can learn to overcome this, and so can you. But it takes a bit of doing.

Consider what is happening from a psychobiological perspective. When you are newly attracted to a potential partner, as we saw in the last chapter, your brain function becomes altered. For one thing, your primitives become activated. In addition to keeping you inebriated so you can fall in love, they are hyperalert for possible dangers. One of the main primitives, the *amygdala*, is constantly scanning your environment for dangerous faces, voices, and movements as well as for dangerous words and phrases. It's the alarm system that signals the stress response that occurs whenever we experience performance anxiety of any sort.

For example, suppose you tell a joke to your new date. As you are delivering the punch line, your amygdala starts to take in and

48

process data showing that the corners of your date's mouth appear set when you expected them to be rising into a smile. His eyes are narrowed. Little alarm bells go off in your brain. Your primitives operate in a primarily preverbal mode, so they aren't equipped to analyze why your date isn't getting the joke. But they are equipped to let you know you are in danger of making a fool of yourself.

But that's not all. Your ambassadors are also out in force. Their intention is to dampen down the alarms set off by your primitives. Acting like what you might term neuroaccountants, your *anterior cingulate* and *orbital frontal cortex* are good at accounting for any mistakes you make and correcting them. When your joke falls flat, for example, your ambassadors may start rattling off possible causes: "Does he think I'm boring? Unsophisticated? Was the joke a bit off-color?" To correct the problem and get your performance back on track, they will dish out advice: "Change the topic. Talk about something less risky! Fast!" As long as they think you might be in some sort of emotional hot water, your ambassadors don't rest. Immediately, they get busy planning for and predicting your next social error—which by the way, further activates your primitives. And thus you have a loop between your ambassadors and primitives that keeps you trapped in what we commonly call *performance anxiety*.

All this activity by your ambassadors may sound like a good thing, but unfortunately it tends to tie up a lot of the mental resources required for you to act naturally and be yourself. Being yourself is a tall order when you are nervous. Olympic athletes and performers know all about this problem. Even though the brain has good intentions, overinvolvement on its part can interfere with performance.

On a date, you are going to make mistakes. You are going to sound and act nervous. This is all par for the course. The good news is that I'm going to help you learn how to use psychobiological techniques to battle these natural performance issues.

STAYING IN THE SAFETY ZONE

The psychobiological techniques I'll recommend are designed to keep you in the safety zone. By that, I mean that their underlying strategy is to move you toward secure functioning in your potential new relationship. The secret to battling performance anxiety on a date is to keep yourself feeling safe and secure.

Stephen Porges (2011), a well-known researcher, describes three strategies the nervous system resorts to in social situations. The first he calls *safety* mode. This involves having control over the breath and the ability to maintain eye contact, modulate the voice, and communicate in a relaxed and friendly manner. In this mode, says Porges, your brain operates optimally and you feel safe even in a stressful interaction, such as a first date. You are able to think before you act, and keep yourself and your partner calm. If a joke seems to be heading south, no problem: you adjust your presentation and maintain your composure. The date is going well.

If this first strategy fails, the nervous system shifts to *danger* mode. This is also known as *fight or flight* because those are your two main options when you no longer feel safe. Fight or flight is marked by lip smacking due to a dry mouth; cold, sweaty palms; blushing; speaking fast or in a high-pitched tone of voice; and jerky movements of the body, head, and neck. In fight or flight, brain function has been compromised and you lose the ability to remain socially engaged. For example, if you or your partner says something that results in extreme embarrassment, you physically plunge into danger mode.

If even the danger mode fails, your nervous system goes into what Porges describes as *life threat*. You can neither fight nor flee, and that leads to collapse. Signs and symptoms include dizziness, ringing in the ears, nausea, loss of muscle tone, loss of color in the face, and vacancy in the eyes. Speech can become difficult, and the voice gets very low and slow. The experience of shame, for example, can trigger this reaction.

Now, I'm not trying to scare you. I'm not suggesting you should expect to experience life threat on your average first date. However, if you or your partner has undergone traumatic experiences at some stage of life, symptoms can emerge during the stress of a new dating situation. In most cases, though, these will be momentary and nothing that requires immediate professional help.

So, why is this important? Because although these modes happen automatically within your nervous system, you have the power to regulate them yourself, at least to a certain extent. You can intentionally work to put yourself, and keep yourself, in the safety zone. The ability to do this is vital if you want to put your best foot forward on a date.

In addition to staying calm yourself, you want to begin to assess a potential partner's ability to remain engaged with you, even in difficult moments, as well as to help relax and calm you down in such moments. It is only fair that in a relationship, your partner be able to soothe you when you get too excited, and you must be able to soothe him or her, as well. To make a relationship work over the long haul, you will both have to be good at this. Even your first few dates are not too soon to start paying attention to how safe you feel with each other.

CALMING YOUR OWN NERVES

Perhaps the most effective technique for keeping yourself calm is paying careful attention to the ups and downs of your own nervous system. This form of awareness is a key element of the practice known as *mindfulness*. Mindfulness refers to the effort to focus one's attention on the details of one's moment-to-moment experience. All the senses—smell, taste, touch, and sight—are involved. Each sense conveys valuable information about what is going on within you. Taken together, these cues let you know at any moment where you are on the inner continuum that runs from calm to chaotic. Not only that, you can use the constant flow of information as feedback to help you move yourself closer to calm on that continuum.

The trick is to observe without judgment or distraction. If you notice that you are less calm than you would like to be, for instance, you don't make it worse by faulting yourself. You watch your experience as if you were an impartial observer. Moreover, you don't let yourself become distracted. It is easy to get caught up in other thoughts or external stimuli and stop paying attention to the stream of cues from your nervous system. This basic practice of mindfulness dates back centuries within the Buddhist tradition, but has been applied in recent decades by psychologists and others for its health benefits.

EXERCISE: MINDFUL BREATH

One of the simplest yet most potent mindfulness techniques is simply to watch your own breath. If you have never tried this before, I suggest you find a quiet place and time where you can sit by yourself and mentally put aside your regular activities. I'm not talking about a long time. Five minutes is all you need. This simple form of mindfulness practice serves as a great foundation for the techniques you will learn in the rest of this book.

1. Sit comfortably, with your back straight but not rigid, and close your eyes.

2. Take a couple of deep breaths, exhaling each fully, to relax yourself.

3. Now let your breath flow at its natural pace. Place your full attention on your breath, watching as it goes in and goes out. Don't do anything to alter its flow. Just watch.

4. Thoughts may arise that cause you to turn your attention away from your breath. Each time you notice this happening, just calmly return your focus to your breath.

5. After five minutes (or however long you practice mindful breathing), notice how you feel. In particular, notice if you feel more relaxed, more comfortable in your body, more at ease.

This exercise is a good way to begin learning to regulate your own nervous system. After you become comfortable doing it with eyes closed and by yourself, practice doing it with your eyes open and in the company of others.

I teach mindfulness techniques to couples as a way to keep each other on an even keel over the long run in their relationship. If one partner is feeling anxious, for example, the other learns how to respond in a soothing manner so the two can regain their equilibrium together. This same technique is also extremely useful in dating situations. One difference, of course, is that you and your date don't yet know each other well, and wouldn't be expected to regulate each other's nervous systems. But you can begin by carefully observing and then regulating your own system while on a date.

Daniel Siegel (2007), a research pioneer in this field, explains the effectiveness of mindfulness in terms of *neuroplasticity*. In other words, mindfulness enables you to actually change how your nervous system is operating. By consciously directing your attention, you activate the corresponding neurons in your brain. This in turn creates new neural pathways.

For example, suppose you feel anxious during a moment of silence between you and your new date. Instead of immediately saying something to fill the silence—which might only make your anxiety more apparent—you could pay attention to your present-moment sensory experience. According to the findings of neuroscience by Siegel and others, this can alter activity in your brain at a neural level, leading to a new experience in which you no longer feel anxiety under the same conditions.

In fact, Jacqueline Lutz and her Austrian colleagues (2014) demonstrated similar results in a laboratory experiment. They compared the brain scans of two groups of people who viewed photographs with strong emotional content: one group practiced mindfulness and the other group received no mindfulness training. Subjects who practiced mindfulness had less activity in their amygdala and associated areas of the brain after seeing negatively stimulating photographs than did people who had no experience of mindfulness. It is not a great leap to assume that mindfulness would have similar effects in a natural setting outside the laboratory, such as on a date, with a real-life experience rather than a photograph.

The subjects in Lutz's experiment—and others in similar research—practiced a mindfulness meditation. That is, they were trained to watch their experience while sitting with eyes closed. The aspect of mindfulness I stress is less formal. You don't need to close your eyes to be aware of the workings of your nervous system. In fact, closing your eyes when you are feeling performance anxiety is likely to increase your anxiety. Not to mention that if you close your eyes too much during a first date, it will probably ensure that is your last date!

EXERCISE: MINDFULNESS PRACTICE

A good way to learn mindfulness is to practice with a friend. Find a buddy—maybe someone who is not a potential date—who is interested in developing the same skills, and set up a time to practice together. You can consider it your faux date.

1. You can calm your nervous system by mindfully relaxing your muscles. To do this, scan your body from head to toe. Wherever you notice tension, focus your attention on relaxing those muscles. Then resume scanning.

When you notice a new area of tension, relax those muscles, and so on. You and your partner should practice this for a few minutes to make sure you have the hang of it.

2. Now pretend you and your practice partner are on your faux date. Have a casual conversation, and as you interact, scan your body for any new tensions that arise. Notice if your face is tight. Notice your neck and back and chest and hips and legs and hands. Even your fingers and toes. Continually scan for tension, without judging what you notice. Just notice, and then relax any place that feels tense.

3. At the end of your practice date, compare notes with your partner. You can give each other feedback about how nervous or relaxed you each appeared, and how that affected the interaction.

Of course, this kind of practice is not a one-time thing. Like putting a puppy back on the newspaper to train it, you're going to have to paper train your mind by continuously scanning your body for any new tensions that arise, and then letting them go as best you can. You can practice this in many situations in your life: work meetings, sports competitions, classroom discussions, job interviews, with family, and so on. The more you practice, the better prepared you will be on an actual date.

One note of caution: I know I told you to constantly scan your body, but the truth is that you don't want to spend too much time focusing on your body or inner experience during a date. If you do, your eyes will begin to look strange to your partner. You may appear spaced out or disinterested in him or her—not good. In the next chapter, I'll discuss how you can also place your attention on your partner. This will help you compensate for the time you do spend attending to your inner sensory experience and relaxing your muscles.

EXERCISE: SAFE TALK

I'd like you to go on another faux date. In the mindfulness practice exercise, what you were talking about didn't matter. This time, you are going to practice speaking to your buddy specifically about your-self and including topics with varying degrees of safety and threat. The purpose in this case is to get a sense not only of how you feel within yourself but also how you come across while you are speaking about yourself. For example, how easy or hard is it to remain calm as you are speaking? What happens when you feel open and secure? Insecure or defensive?

1. Start by taking a few minutes to calm your nervous sys-tem by mindfully relaxing.

2. Have your buddy interview you. He or she can ask ques-tions about your history, career, failures and successes, hobbies, favorite things, and anything else you might cover on a first date. But at this point, keep the topics light and easy.

3. Answer the questions as clearly as possible. As you are speaking, be mindfully aware of what is happening in your body.

4. Now have your buddy ask you to talk about something about which you are insecure or unsure. It could be a past partner or a family member with whom you have unresolved issues.

5. Again, as you answer, pay attention to what is happening in your body.

6. At the end of your faux date, discuss with your buddy how you felt answering the two sets of questions. What differences did your buddy notice in your face, voice, and body as you responded in each case?

Because the Safe Talk exercise is a faux date, I encourage you to give yourself permission to say whatever you wish, and just observe what happens. Don't judge your experience.

When you take what you have learned about yourself into a real dating situation, you can make informed choices. If you know it is hard for you to talk about, for example, an illness you had, you can choose when and under what conditions you speak about it with a new potential partner. You might choose ahead of time to say, "This is something I find difficult to talk about. I'd like to tell you more about it when we know each other better."

Note that I'm not suggesting you ever talk about your ex or other potentially tense topics on a real first date (as opposed to a faux date). However, these topics will (and should) come up sooner or later in real-life dating, and this exercise is intended to help you prepare for them.

Preparing for a Date

So far, we have considered how you can practice calming your body and mind. You can do this when you are alone, at work, while driving, and of course on a date. You can also apply similar principles ahead of a date. Don't underestimate the impact of the right preparations on how well your date goes.

The night before a date, especially a first date, I suggest going to bed early. You want to feel rested. Some people like to prepare themselves as they fall asleep by imagining a good outcome. For example, you might picture friends and family congratulating you on a successful dating experience. You might picture your date complimenting you on being so natural and relaxed and fun to be with, and picture planning a second date with this person. This strategy of visualizing the future helps regulate your nervous system so you feel confident and at ease.

Another way you can prepare, if you have the time, is to go to the gym ahead of your date. The rush of endorphins you generate through exercise will help you feel energized and not anxious. You can also check in with your support network. For example, reach out to a close friend ahead of time, and plan to touch base after the date in case things go poorly so you will have a soft place to land.

A Mindful Dinner

You can apply the psychobiological approach I have been describing to effectively manage your jitters on a date. To begin with, here is a brief list of some practical dos and don'ts based on what we've been discussing.

- Do scan your body regularly for tensions that arise, and let them go.

- Do notice your thoughts, attend to new resulting tensions that arise in your body, and let them go.

- Don't overthink things ahead of time.

- Don't dwell on anxieties.

- However, don't deny any anxiety you may feel.

- Do get plenty of rest and take the time to prepare yourself before a date.

- Do pay close attention to your inner experience at all times.

- Do pay close attention to your date at all times.

- However, don't focus on your inner experience to the exclusion of your date, or vice versa.

- Do use your senses of sight, hearing, touch, taste, and smell.

Now notice how Raul employs these various principles on his date with Tia. Raul broke up with his girlfriend of seven years three years ago and has not dated since. He met Tia online through a dating service. Both are working professionals in their thirties.

Raul prepares himself for the date by getting a good night's sleep beforehand and going to the gym the morning of the date. On his drive to the restaurant, he listens to music that helps create the mood he wants and begins to tune in to his body. He makes sure not to distract himself with thoughts about the date. He knows his tendency to think too much makes him tense up.

Raul chose a restaurant that has decent lighting and is quiet enough so he and Tia can see and hear each other as fully as possible. When Raul walks in, the host says his date has already arrived. Raul tenses up at the thought that he is late. But he remembers to relax all the muscles of his body, and realizes Tia is simply early.

As he walks toward Tia, Raul takes in as much detail as he can. He is aware that his eyes are transitioning from his far to his near visual stream. Tia is wearing an elegant white dress. She has shoulder-length brown hair with blonde highlights. She has a gold chain with a heart locket around her neck, no rings on her hands, and an analog watch on her right arm. He wonders if she is left-handed. He does not detect any perfume. As he shakes the warm and dry hand she extends, Raul looks into her eyes and smiles. "Hello, Tia," he says.

She greets him, and they remain for a few seconds with hands in contact. Raul relaxes any muscle tension as it arises. He notices a lovely asymmetry in Tia's eyes and nose, then glances down at her body and dress, including her shoes, which are white flats. Scanning her in this way allows him to say naturally, "You look stunning."

After they are seated, he notices Tia lower her eyes momentarily. She appears shier than he expected. "I'm a little nervous," she says. "Are you?"

"Absolutely," he says with a smile. To say anything else would only make her more uncomfortable. It's always easier for two people to be uncomfortable together. "I'm actually a very anxious person," he says candidly. "But, here, put your hand on mine." He extends his hand so she can put hers on it.

"Okay…" she says suspiciously, her hand still on her lap.

"Go ahead. I'll explain," he reassures her. When Tia puts her hand on his, he says, "Warm and dry, just as when I shook it. That tells me you aren't as nervous as you think."

Tia smiles. "Thanks. I guess I'm more at ease with you than I realized."

Again Raul sweeps his body for muscle tension and lets it go as best he can, allowing them to comfortably maintain their hand contact and mutual gaze for a few seconds. "Shall we order?"

"I almost forgot," says Tia, giggling as she withdraws her hand to look at the menu.

Reading this, you might think Raul comes across as a bit unnatural, a bit too controlled. When you first try psychobiological techniques, they can sometimes feel this way. But stick with it. Consider which of the techniques Raul used could work well for you, and experiment with them. The more you practice, the more natural it will feel, until pretty soon it becomes second nature.

FINAL THOUGHTS

Even the most socially skillful of us may experience some performance anxiety when we think about or actually go on a first date. This and the following chapters should help calm that anxiety and give you more confidence so you can have a good time on that first date. I encourage you to keep becoming more aware of how your nervous system functions so you can learn to relax yourself. As one who used to be shy and socially anxious, I can testify that these techniques have worked well for me, both professionally and personally.

The focus in this chapter has been on what you can do for yourself: you can become the master of your own nervous system, rather than let it dictate your experience on a date. In the next chapter, you are going to put the same kinds of psychobiological techniques to use, but this time focused less on your internal experience and more on your date. This will help you determine whether a potential date could be the right partner for you.

CHAPTER 4

Uncovering the Clues to a Good Match

Sherlock Holmes, the nineteenth-century fictional detective, achieved such notoriety that his name is now a common noun in the dictionary. That's convenient, because in this chapter I'm going to ask you to become a sherlock on your dates. As a sherlock, you can apply the psychobiological approach described in the last chapter to help you learn more about your potential partner.

In chapter 2, we talked about three phases of vetting. Let me recapitulate. In the initial screening phase, you check a potential partner for basic appropriateness. We discussed this using the example of Milo, whose fog of infatuation was so dense he failed to determine that Kathy was unlikely to be a good match. It would not have taken much sleuthing for Milo to see that she was not interested in a serious relationship. Like the initial phase, the phase of ongoing assessment is something you can do yourself. This phase involves becoming a sherlock and, as such, is much more involved than the initial screening. The second phase, which we discussed in chapter 2, is deeper vetting done by family and friends.

You may think of the second aspect as the true vetting process, but I don't want you to minimize the amount of evaluation you can perform yourself while dating. Don't forget that the first person in the vetting hierarchy is *you*. Others can help and even save you with their more distant perspective, but you are the one with boots on the ground. Bottom line: when you apply a psychobiological approach, you have a lot more information at your fingertips. In this chapter, I will show you how to obtain that information as well as how to put it to good use on a date.

BECOME A SHERLOCK

As a sherlock, you can gather a wealth of information about your partner. Speaking about the average person, the original Sherlock famously said, "You see, but you do not observe. The distinction is clear." Even though we commonly use these two verbs interchangeably, observing is a more involved process. Seeing is simply the automatic function of a healthy eye. Observing, however, is a process that requires a fully operational brain. As a sherlock, your power of observation includes more than sight: bringing your other senses to bear, as well as your verbal abilities, allows you to get more complete information. You notice details you would otherwise miss—perhaps details that other people might dismiss as inconsequential. Moreover, you can ask appropriate questions to find out more and to fill in the blanks.

Sherlock Holmes was known for his sharp use of deductive reasoning to make the most of his observations, and you, too, can put the information you gather to good use by applying Sherlockian logic. By that, I mean you can use this information as part of the process of evaluating a potential partner. In this way, you can balance the impetuous impulses of your primitives with a more disciplined evaluation.

There are other benefits to becoming a sherlock, as well. For one, focusing outward on your partner saves you from appearing to be navel gazing on a date. Self-obsession is a turnoff. Moreover, sherlocking is a mindful activity. As such, its effect on you is very similar to that of close attention to your own internal experience. Both have a calming effect on your nervous system. Perhaps most importantly, careful attention to your partner helps him or her feel appreciated and valued and secure in your presence. Everyone likes to be the center of attention. It feels good.

I should say at this point that if your potential partner gets the impression you are investigating, interrogating, or otherwise intruding on him or her, this will likely be your last date. Nobody likes to feel as if he or she is being looked at under a microscope. Unfortunately, many people come on too strong on their first dates, only to lose the other person's interest.

So, bottom line: don't overdo it. Your job is to pick up as much information as you can without appearing as though you're doing that. Remember to keep relaxing your body and letting go of muscle tension; this will help you come across as interested, engaged, open, and inviting. Which, after all, is what you really are. Right?

OBSERVING THE NONVERBAL CLUES

It is easy to go into a date—or any situation—intending to be alert, only to become distracted in the moment or end up observing in a very generalized manner. Afterward, the thought is "Now, what was I going to look for...?" With this in mind, I have put together a list of the kinds of things you want to observe in your potential partner on a date. To begin with, I've limited these to nonverbal clues. Trying to observe everything at the same time can result in overlooking important details, so I suggest you practice with these first.

- Eyes (color, pupils that are large and open or small and constricted, any small muscle movements around the eyes)

- Eye contact (avoidance of, wandering eyes, staring, present and friendly)

- Mouth (lip corners up or down, closed or tight, open or relaxed)

- Facial expression (under- or overexpressive)

- Facial coloring (pallor, blushing)

- Posture (straight, hunched, tilted)

- Movements and gestures (fidgety and jerky or smooth and relaxed, foot tapping, hair twirling)

- Hair (color, layers, curly or straight, which side of the head the hair is parted)

- Skin (lines on the forehead or around the eyes or mouth, laugh lines, crows' feet, washed out)

- Left-handed or right-handed

- Body (weight, height, shape)

- Scent (perfume, shampoo, body, breath)

- Clothing and accessories (casual or dressy, jewelry, piercings, tattoos)

- Voice (loud or soft, modulated tone or flat)

- Laughter (giggly, raucous, frequency, sincerity)

- Smile (true, fake, frequency)

This is only a partial list, of course. The idea is that you familiarize yourself with the list ahead of time so your brain is primed, so to speak, then pay attention to what you see moment to moment on the date.

This kind of close observation only works if it is nonjudgmental. You don't want to be constantly weighing the good and bad points of your date, as if you were keeping score. Thinking "I like this about you, I don't like that" is not conducive to enjoying yourself as you get to know someone, much as judging yourself is a sure way to become distracted. Plus your potential partner will notice your judgments written all over your face. You are being watched and observed, too.

But don't worry, you'll have plenty of opportunity after the date is over to weigh all the information you have taken in, without judgment, in the moment.

As you perfect your powers of observation, you can start to use the clues you are picking up in the moment to help you be more responsive to your date. For example, if you notice your date fidgeting when you ask about his upcoming bar exam, you might want to steer away from that topic. Or if your date is squinting, you might offer to adjust the nearby window blinds. In other words, your careful observation allows you to adjust your own behavior in ways you might not if you weren't paying such close attention.

I have emphasized nonverbal communication here not so much because it is more important, but because it is more often overlooked. However, I don't want you to get the impression that how you and your potential partner speak to each other doesn't matter. Obviously it is crucial. Most of the rest of the book focuses heavily on what you can say and how you can say it, as well as how to listen to what your date says so that you can build a foundation of positive communication. So let's start with the basics.

INTERVIEWING A POTENTIAL PARTNER

As is the case with nonverbal clues, the verbal clues you pick up in conversation are invaluable in helping you determine whether your potential partner is a good match. Most of us probably think about the kinds of questions that can be asked to glean as much information as possible about a potential partner. This is important. And it is a good place to begin.

There are, of course, some obvious, predictable topics:

- Where were you born?

- Do you have brothers and sisters?

- What kind of work do you do?

- How long have you been at your job?

- What is your favorite color?

I don't mean to denigrate these questions, because all of them can yield good information. Some are especially appropriate for the initial screening phase when you are looking for very basic information and want to help your date relax. For example, you may want to establish early on whether an individual is financially secure and responsible. Of course, you want to do so in a manner that does not appear threatening.

In any case, limiting yourself to the obvious and predictable as you get to know a potential partner is a surefire formula for a boring date. You want to perfect the art of mixing in more interesting questions that will bring to light more about your partner, things you might not learn if you stick to the obvious questions. For instance, you don't just want to know how many brothers and sisters your date may have; you want to know his or her birth order and if he or she is close to these siblings. Knowing about the quality of their relationship can give you some clues about the kind of family life you might expect with this person if you end up together. In the chapters that follow, you will learn more about how to get to know your potential partner, but for now here are some questions you can use:

- What kinds of things did your family do together when you were a kid?

- Who has had the biggest impact on your life?

- Who was your favorite teacher?

- If you could go anywhere in the world, where would you go?

- What is your favorite book?

- What is your favorite Sunday morning activity?

- What is the best present anyone ever gave you?

- What would you like your life to be like in ten years?

- What do you find most scary about dating?

- What are you most interested in knowing about me?

When you are asking questions such as these, the other half of the equation is listening to the answers. You can ask the most intriguing questions in the world, but the answers will be only minimally useful for assessing a partner if you don't know how to listen carefully and pay close attention. That includes listening between the lines. As a sherlock, you always want to observe your potential partner's nonverbal clues as he or she speaks, as well as listen for the subtle verbal clues. The next exercise is designed to help you do this.

EXERCISE: LISTENING BETWEEN THE LINES

While your date is speaking—either in response to your questions or simply telling you something without prompting—pay attention to the subtle clues. In other words, pay attention to the tone and tenor of the speech, as well as to the context. Ask yourself as you listen to your date:

- Does your date tell you too little?

- Does your date give you too much information?

- Does your date lead you astray or give you false information?

- Does your date become tangential and take the conversation all over the place?

- Does your date talk about people or events for which there has been no previous introduction?

- Does your date suddenly pause or slow down for no apparent reason?

When you listen between the lines in this manner, you will not only learn about the facts of your potential partner's life, as well as his or her thoughts and feelings, you will also get some clues to how this individual functions in a relationship. We will explore this more fully in the coming chapters.

GLEANING FROM THE CLUES

What we have covered thus far in this chapter might be considered "Sherlocking 101." If you can be alert and present in the moment on your date, both observing and managing your own internal experience, and observing your partner, you should be in great shape. You will put yourself in the best position to be relaxed and have fun, and just see what can happen with your potential new partner.

However, I don't want to give the impression that this is all there is to psychobiological techniques. In fact, as you learn more about this approach, you will see both how versatile and how powerful it can be. I'd like to give you a couple of examples in which partners used psychobiological techniques effectively early on during the dating process to resolve a confusing or complex set of clues that would have thrown most people.

Tobin and Michael are on their first date at a café. As Tobin carefully observes Michael, he notices Michael's eyes frequently wander across the room. Every time someone enters, Michael looks over. It seems a bit rude. But Tobin wants to give his date the benefit of the doubt, so he says, "Excuse me, are you expecting someone?"

Michael gives a little jump. "Me? No. Why do you ask?"

"Well, I noticed you seem to be watching the door."

"Not at all," says Michael. "I didn't realize I was doing that."

As their date progresses, Michael no longer watches the door, but Tobin has trouble deciphering the clues on his face. He doesn't smile much, and it is hard to tell if he is bored or aloof or actually just content. Tobin nonetheless finds Michael very attractive, so he suggests a second date in a more private location. At that time, Michael comes across as animated and expressive and shows his great sense of humor. He also confesses to Tobin that he came out to his family only a few months ago, and that their date at the café had been a first for him.

As human beings, we require clear signals from another person's face and voice in order to feel that everything is okay between us. Whether we do it consciously, or just unconsciously, we search for signals to let us know we are on the right track, getting along, and understanding one another. If someone has a minimally expressive face, as in Michael's case, we may feel anxious and uncertain around that person. When we don't have enough information about someone, the tendency is to fill in the blanks ourselves. Under stress—which we often feel while dating—we rarely assume the positive; we automatically think there's something wrong.

Tobin's is a great example of how careful observation can save a first date that otherwise might have gone south. Where someone else might have taken offense or become suspicious, he was able to glean from the clues he had that Michael was worth a "second look." His hunch bore out when he discovered that Michael was just overly nervous—with good cause—on their first date.

Sleuthing can also work the other way; that is, you can use the clues you find to save you from a potential disaster.

Take the example of Evelyn and Jack. After their first date, which went well, Evelyn invited him to go biking with her a few days later. After riding ten miles, they went back to her apartment to cool off.

Thus far, Evelyn has paid special attention to how Jack's face looks when he is happy, when he is sad, and when he talks about something that makes him angry. She is getting a baseline of his facial expressions, gestures, and vocal patterns. Of course, it is all new at this point, but she already recognizes enough to notice he is different now, as they sit in her living room sipping iced tea. He isn't looking her in the eye, as he did before, and seems ill at ease.

"So how are you feeling?" she asks.

"Fine," says Jack, picking up a book on the coffee table, still not meeting her eyes. "That was a fantastic workout."

Evelyn feels her body getting hot as she reads his denial as just that—denial. She can tell something is amiss, though she can't put her finger on it. She continues to pay close attention, while changing the subject to something less confrontational. "So, tell me about your week."

"It's been weird, actually." Jack pauses. "It's hard to explain. What about you? How was your week?"

Evelyn is frustrated that he has blocked her, but she starts to talk about her job as a bookkeeper. In the back of her mind, she wonders what he might be hiding.

Without warning, Jack interrupts her midsentence: "Are you dating anyone else?"

Evelyn is caught off guard. "Uh, no," she says, then adds, wondering if this is really an admission on his part, "Are you?"

"As a matter of fact, a girl I used to see contacted me this week. It was weird. We haven't seen each other in six months."

Evelyn nods. The fact that he said "weird" again tells her this is the information he was withholding. Now she wonders how honest he is being with her. "Is it serious?" she asks.

"Nah, not at all." Jack replies, with a high-pitched laugh that suggests to Evelyn he is not being straight up. "Dating you makes everyone else seem like nothing. You're so perfect!"

Evelyn feels her stomach tighten as he calls her "perfect." It doesn't ring true. Her own internal clues, combined with Jack's lack of eye contact and his denial, make it increasingly clear to Evelyn that she may not be able to trust this man. Just as he lurches forward to plant a kiss on her lips, she puts out her hand to stop him.

"Nope," she says, "not okay."

She makes it clear that she is no longer interested in dating him. The main reason is not that he's dating someone else. That, she thinks, is normal when people are dating a lot. His inability to be forthcoming with her is what turns her off.

Here we have a situation where Evelyn was able to use her sleuthing ability to identify a problem before it was too late. She picked up enough relevant clues to figure out in time that Jack was most likely lying to her. Had she been less aware, she might have continued into a relationship in which she was deceived in hurtful ways. You might say, well, she didn't have proof that he was lying or that he was going to cheat on her. No, she didn't. But in cases like this, where many psychobiological signals converge, it is usually better to be safe than sorry. At a minimum, she would be advised to take a step back and gather more information—for example, if they talk on the phone, noticing his tone of voice as they discuss what happened between them—before going on more dates.

FINAL THOUGHTS

Remember that at the beginning of the dating process, everyone is trying to sell himself or herself, including you. We all want to be liked. When people really want something, they tend to inadvertently show unattractive facets of themselves while under pressure. This is true if you are an Olympic skater trying to give your best performance, a politician trying to look good during a debate, or a celebrity trying to protect your public image on camera. Our automatic brains—our primitives—are even more automatic when we are under stress. As you begin to practice the psychobiological techniques I have described, please cut yourself—and your date—some slack. The chance that one or both of you will do or say something foolish at some point is pretty high.

For these reasons, I describe this sherlocking phase as one of ongoing assessment. It isn't something you do once or twice and come to a quick conclusion—unless, of course, you discover something about your potential partner you consider a deal breaker. In that case, your efforts have paid off early, and you act accordingly. Otherwise, you continue observing and gathering information. And, hopefully, you enjoy your dates, knowing you have new skills to help you feel more assured of making a good match and getting what you really want in a relationship.

CHAPTER 5

Know Yourself, Know Your Partner

By now you are getting the hang of the psychobiological approach to dating. You have a sense of the ingredients of your attraction and also know a bit about your mutual interests, as well as your differences. You have begun the vetting process in earnest. Maybe you have brought him or her to meet a friend or two. No alarm bells have gone off to let you know this is not the partner for you. For the moment, you have a green light.

Now for a sobering idea. I believe that it takes approximately one year to get to know someone well enough to have any certainty about whether you can be partners over the long term. That is, before you buy in to a true commitment. Before that, you don't know enough about that person or about yourself with that person. The bloom is still on the rose. I don't say this to be discouraging. In fact, if you consider it alongside Mark Twain's comment to the effect that a couple can't know what real love is until they've been married for a quarter century, one year is encouraging.

This chapter, therefore, covers what you can expect to focus on throughout the entire first year of dating your new potential partner. We could say that on the first date or two, you have essentially been window-shopping. You have gotten a sense of what you are looking for and what attracts you. Now, after those first couple of dates, you are going to walk into the store and decide whether or not you want to purchase that to which you are attracted and actually bring it home with you.

You might think I'm being a bit crass to speak about relationships as if they're some form of financial transaction. Of course they're not. But I like this metaphor because I think it highlights how our brains work as we go through the series of decisions—many of them unconscious—in the process of selecting a partner. In this chapter, I will share with you more about how this works, and specifically what I think you need to know about the person you're dating. I am talking about aspects of your date's personality and habits that he or she may not even know about himself or herself. This can get tricky, so we will spend the next several chapters on it.

THINGS TO KNOW BEFORE YOU BUY

Why does it take so long to get to know another person? Human beings are complex creatures. If someone you meet tries to sell you "simple," don't buy. There's no such thing. Does that mean you should go with somebody who claims on the first date to be very complex? I wouldn't buy that, either. Admitting in the early stages of dating that you're a complex or difficult person is likely to be self-defeating. At the same time, saying you are easy to be with is downright misleading.

Your primitives, as we discussed already, act on impulse. They want to have everything operating on automatic. That means they naturally move fast, without leaving time for much thought or premeditation. This is a normal neurological process, and helpful under many circumstances, but it can be a big problem during courtship. To really learn about another person, you have to interact with him or her over time. For example, when you get into a fight with that person—which eventually you will do, trust me—you'll be able to see what it's like to interact during conflict. You need to know what your potential partner is like under stress in various situations. During courtship, both individuals are putting their best feet forward, but you must also see each other at your worst. If you don't, you won't know if you can accept each other as you are when the going gets tough.

I don't mean to be rigid about taking one year to know another person. There is no rule that you are not allowed to get married within the first year. Couples do it, and it works for them. My point is simply that it takes time to really know your partner, and that this auditioning is best done before marriage. If you don't take the time, your risk of failure rises significantly.

In the first chapter, I asked you to describe your ideal partner. You might want to revisit that list now because you are going to build upon it. Through the eyes of our buying metaphor, that list represents the thoughts and hopes you have as you—for example—peer into the showroom window and check out that new car. You like that it's red, you like the sticker price, and you like whatever else you can see from that vantage point. But you have no idea what it feels like to get behind the wheel and take a test drive. Obviously, the test-drive phase of dating is more complex than that of buying a car. But you get my point.

How do you go about this process? Fortunately, attachment theory offers a highly effective means for better understanding what you are buying. When you go to buy a car—if you will bear with me in prolonging this metaphor—you don't just buy "a car"; you pay attention to its type, or model. When it comes to relationships, the "types" you want to attend to are based on a person's sense of safety and security.

THE THREE ATTACHMENT TYPES

Psychologists have devised ways to distinguish among the main attachment types. In the second half of the last century, Mary Ainsworth and colleagues (1971) set up what she called the "Strange Situation," in which researchers observe a child playing, first in a parent's presence and then with a stranger. It turned out that secure and insecure children react very differently when the parent leaves and later returns.

Secure children aren't too bothered by their parent's absence because they feel secure in the relationship. Some insecure children, on the other hand, show almost no distress when their parent leaves, but when the parent returns, they continue to avoid or ignore the parent. In fact, the parent typically does the same thing: the parent may not even pick up or greet the child. Because the parent does not value closeness, the child stops seeking it and even regards it as intrusive. It is as if the child is saying, "What do you want now?!" Other insecure children respond by clinging. They get very upset when the parent leaves, and may even try to stop the parent. When the parent does return, they may express anger at the parent for seemingly abandoning them. In this case, the parent has reacted ambivalently to the child, perhaps by demonstrating closeness at some times and by withholding it at other times. As a result, the child feels emotionally confused and insecure.

I have described this research in detail because, not only is it fascinating, but it has set the stage for what we now know about the importance of secure functioning in adult relationships. (If you are interested, you can find videos of the Strange Situation online.) I'm not suggesting you need to know how you would have responded as a child. Rather, take this research on attachment as the groundwork for how adults function in relationships. Individuals who grew up in a secure environment are basically secure in their adult relationships. Others did not receive a secure upbringing and so relate through a veil of insecurity that can cause them to remain distant from a partner or bring ambivalence to the relationship.

ANCHOR, ISLAND, AND WAVE

Psychologists use terms such as *securely attached*, *insecurely avoidant*, and *insecurely ambivalent* to describe the main attachment styles. These correspond to the three types of responses to the Strange Situation that I just described. I prefer to use the simpler terms *anchor, island,* and *wave.* These are the three predominant styles, and if you have a basic understanding of them, you will be at an advantage during the buying phase of relationships as you get to know your new partner.

Each of the three types has different strengths, as you can see from Table 5.1. In the three chapters that follow, we will discuss each type in detail. For now, however, you can compare the strengths listed here and can get a sense of which type might best describe you.

Table 5.1 The Three Attachment Types

Type	Strengths
Anchor	Secure as individuals Willing to commit and fully share with another Generally happy people Adapt easily to the needs of the moment
Island	Independent and self-reliant Take good care of themselves Productive and creative, especially when given space Low maintenance
Wave	Generous and giving Focused on taking care of others Happiest when around other people Able to see both sides of an issue

THE STYLES OF RELATING IN ACTION

You don't have to wait until you're in a full-blown relationship to recognize these differences in style. They come into play even in the earliest phases of dating.

Consider Fran and Lester, both in their thirties. Now they are on their third date. Fran, a writer for a popular news magazine, canceled once due to a deadline, and then just this afternoon asked to move their date from 6 p.m. to 8 p.m. because she was running late. Lester, a psychiatric aide, is feeling unsettled by these cancellations and postponements. He wonders if Fran is really interested.

Both said their first date was good. Fran was impressed by Lester's sensitivity, his interest in her, and his sense of humor. Lester was taken by Fran's confidence, intelligence, and beauty. Lester was married once, but his wife left him after a year because she said he was too needy. He feels he has finished mourning his marriage and is ready to move on. Fran, on the other hand, has never been married. She broke up with her previous boyfriend because he felt she kept choosing her career over their relationship.

We meet them on their date at a restaurant. Lester is already seated when Fran breezes in, a full twenty minutes late. She apologizes and reaches out to hug him. She expects him to rise and hug her in return, but he stays seated, so the hug is rather lopsided.

"Fran," he says, keeping his voice calm so she won't detect his underlying annoyance, "I see your work is really demanding."

"Yeah." Fran slides into her chair and quickly scans the menu. She mumbles something about choosing between two dishes, then looks up at Lester. "I'm starved!"

He won't let her change the topic. But it is getting harder to sound calm. "Is this going to happen often?" he demands.

"Is what going to happen?"

Does she really think her behavior is okay? he wonders. Or maybe she's just that oblivious. "Are you always going to cancel at the last minute because of work?"

Fran has a sudden flash of her last boyfriend, who made an issue of the same thing. "Why do you ask?" she says defensively.

Lester backs off when he senses her irritation. He recalls his wife saying he was too clingy, that he didn't give her the space she needed. "No reason," he says. "Just curious."

The waiter comes over and they order. But Lester is still ill at ease, so he feels compelled to return to his earlier point. "Like I said, last week you had to cancel. Will that happen often?"

Fran frowns. She thought they had gotten past that point. "Are you saying that's a worry for you?" she counters.

"What?" Lester is uncomfortable that she has turned the question back on him and doesn't want her to think he's a complainer. So he deflects with another question.

Fran thinks she was being clear, but apparently she wasn't. She tries to clarify. After all, she thinks, if Lester can't handle everything about her, maybe they should end the relationship before it gets ugly. "Do you get upset by things like having to cancel at the last minute?" she asks, then adds, "I'm sorry I had to do that. But, yes, it happens from time to time."

Lester repeats his earlier position. "No worries. I was just curious."

"Well," Fran says, not buying his stance at all, and now more strongly suspecting Lester will be way too high maintenance for her comfort level in relationships. "I think you're more than curious. You sound like it really bothered you when I cancelled."

"Not bothered exactly." Lester scrambles to salvage the situation. He feels almost nauseated by the thought that this beautiful and intelligent woman is about to put a quick end to their budding romance. Instinctively, he thinks that if he can appear more like her, he can repair the damage. "Hey," he says with a high-pitched laugh, "I get busy, too! There will be times when I have to cancel on you."

This new couple are beginning to recognize features in each other that are perceived as potentially threatening. Lester is seen as overly clingy and needy, Fran as overly distancing and work focused. They can't know for sure that these perceived characteristics are accurate. But because our brain is always matching novel experiences with known or remembered experiences, they will be predisposed to react to what they think they recognize as familiar in each other. This can quickly lead to a downward spiral as they confirm their worst fears about each other. As we saw, Fran was already contemplating the end of their relationship. It could easily be over before they reach dessert.

What Lester and Fran don't have is any knowledge about styles of relating. If Lester recognized Fran as having what I refer to as the island style of relating, and she recognized him as having what I call the wave style, their relationship might have a fighting chance. He could think, "Okay, I understand where she's coming from. I don't have to take this personally. As an island, she is naturally going to assert her need to feel independent. If we want to be in a relationship, we can learn to work together on that." And Fran could have parallel thoughts about him, rather than automatically foresee the end of the relationship. She could think, "As a wave, he has a tendency to seem needy, especially to someone like me, who's oriented toward my own freedom. But I like so many other things about him. It would be stupid to dump him without giving this a fair shot." Moreover, as their relationship progresses, actually speaking to each other about their respective attachment types could help them learn to deal more effectively with each other.

WHAT YOU ARE SELLING

A long-term relationship is a pact of one sort or another between two people. Even during the early dating stage, it's not too soon to start thinking about what kind of pact you want—not just in terms of what you want to *get* from your partner but also in terms of what you have to *offer*. In other words, not just what you want to buy, but what you have to sell.

Basically, what you sell is YOU. As we have just seen, one important aspect of what you bring to a relationship is your style of relating. In the next three chapters, we are going to look closely at each of the three main styles. But first there is something even more fundamental: your own level of honesty and awareness about what you're selling. I meet too many people who believe they're selling something other than what they are really selling.

Lola and Rae met through mutual friends a few weeks ago. When she learns Rae rarely goes out to eat, Lola offers to take her somewhere nice. "My treat," she says. "Where would you like to go?"

"Anywhere is fine," Rae says.

Lola describes several places, indicating what Rae might like about each.

Rae listens, then says, "You pick."

Lola chooses a place where they can watch the sun set while they dine, and Rae agrees to the date. However, although being invited to a nice restaurant makes her feel special, Rae is deeply worried that Lola will think she doesn't measure up and will reject her.

As they drive up to the restaurant, Rae suddenly mentions a movie she recently downloaded. Instead of getting out of the car, she suggests they go to her apartment to watch it.

Lola looks confused. "Now? I thought we came here for dinner."

Rae stares at the valet parking. "This place is elegant," she says. "I'm not dressed for it."

Lola laughs. "Don't worry, it's casual. Anyway, you're totally cute!" She moves to open the car door.

Rae doesn't budge. "Are you saying you don't want to come to my apartment?"

Lola frowns. "I never said that."

Rae reacts as she sees Lola frown. Suddenly she worries that she has spoiled the date. "I'm sorry," she says quickly. "You offered to treat, and I've offended you. It's just that I'm a really spontaneous person. I know I can come across as too easygoing, too much of a free spirit."

As you hear Rae defend herself in this way, you are probably as confused as Lola was. Easygoing? Free spirit? She may have said, "Anywhere is fine," but clearly this is a woman who has no idea how she comes off to others.

You may question whether anyone would really give such an off-base self-description. But in my experience, people often misrepresent themselves—knowingly and unknowingly—in small or big ways. We have ideas about ourselves that are quite different from the ways we actually appear to others. Trying to sell yourself as something other than what you are as you begin a dating relationship can get you into hot water.

So the first step is to know who you are.

Obviously, honesty is required. Brutal honesty, at times. For example, Rae could have said, "I get uncomfortable in fancy places. It brings up my insecurities. It's a bit embarrassing to admit this, but I'm saying it because I'd really like to get to know you. How would you feel about meeting in a more relaxed setting before we go out for dinner?" Of course, this presupposes that she is aware of these aspects of her personality, and not hiding behind the image of a free spirit. After you have learned more about anchors, islands, and waves, you may want to come back and speculate on which types Lola and Rae represent.

For now, you can begin to address the question of self-knowledge as one key aspect of the dating process. I'm not talking about necessarily undergoing psychoanalysis or revisiting your entire childhood. However, who you are is a product of everything that has happened to you, and it is important to understand this basic principle. You have been influenced by every important person in your life, as well as some who might not have seemed so important in the moment. What you believe relationships should be like and what relationships mean to you also come from other people. You did not make up these ideas and values yourself. They were consolidated for you early in childhood.

You may not like hearing this. We tend to prefer to think our ideas and beliefs are our own creations. But this is not what attachment theory tells us. Decades of research have established that the qualities of our earliest relationships with our primary caregivers may set us on a course for life—one way or another. In a nutshell, if you had a secure, attentive, loving relationship at a young age, then you will likely be wired for secure, loving relationships as an adult. If you didn't have that kind of protected, emotionally stable situation, then you are at greater risk for forming insecure adult relationships. I'm not saying you can't have wonderful, satisfying, and enduring relationships. But you may have to work harder at it.

EXERCISE: YOUR SELLING POINTS

As a means toward knowing yourself, I suggest you make a list of all the qualities you have to offer a partner. Much like the list you made in the first chapter, of the qualities your ideal partner would have, this list can be just your positive selling points. Don't worry; we'll get to your other qualities next.

To help you create your list of selling points, here are some categories:

1. Your physical attributes

2. Your personality traits

3. Your skills and abilities

4. Your interests and hobbies

5. Your outlook on life and worldview

6. Your moral and spiritual beliefs

At this point, you may wish to compare the selling points you identified in this exercise with the qualities you listed for your ideal partner, in chapter 1. Note that the goal here is not to have lists that are identical. As I've said, you aren't looking for a clone. However, knowing who you are is vital to finding someone who is appropriate for you. In the dating world, unless you know who you are and what you're selling, you cannot really be clear about what you want to buy.

Now for the more difficult part. Knowing yourself would not be complete if you focused only on your great selling points. As you begin a relationship, you need to be aware of everything you bring to the table. This doesn't mean that you have to walk in with a digital slideshow of your assets and liabilities. What I am talking about is having an awareness of your qualities so that you can be honest with your potential partner and can work with these qualities as they arise.

EXERCISE: WHAT YOU BRING

The following list has two sets of ten statements: (1) what you think of yourself, and (2) what others think of you. Go through the lists and make note of which statements you agree with. You don't have to mark the book. No one needs to know what your answers are. The only rule is that you must be honest. If you're not honest, this exercise will be meaningless.

I	II
I tend to be needy.	Others think I'm needy.
I tend to be highly emotional.	Others think I'm highly emotional.
I tend to be clingy.	Others think I'm clingy.
I tend not to be affectionate.	Others think I am not affectionate.
I tend to talk a lot.	Others think I talk a lot.
I tend to be distant.	Others think I'm distant.
I tend to avoid conflict.	Others think I avoid conflict.
I tend to argue a lot.	Others think I argue a lot.
I tend to be bossy.	Others think I'm bossy.
I tend to get my way.	Others think I tend to get my way.

Now consider your answers to the exercise. A number of patterns are possible. One possibility is that you didn't agree with any of the statements. If this is your honest and true response, I say great. You will have an easy time bonding with a partner. Another possibility is that you checked an equal number of statements on both lists. Depending on how many items you checked, that might make for some difficulties as you date. But the good news is that you are going into any relationship alert to whatever challenges you meet.

The other possibility is that you checked more items in one column than in the other. If you checked more items in column 1, I would be concerned. You might think this is a good thing because you are skilled at hiding some of your challenging qualities. Not so fast. That might work in some situations in life, but it won't work in the world of relationships. Sooner or later, it will blow up in your face because you can't hide much for long from a full-time partner. If you checked more statements in column 2, I would be even more concerned. In this case, you feel other people are falsely blaming you for qualities you don't believe you have. This is a recipe for disaster for the simple reason that those other people are most likely better judges of you than you are of yourself.

Bottom line: When it comes to knowing yourself and what you bring to a relationship, two things are essential. First, it is just as important to know your weaknesses as to know your strengths. Second, knowing the impact your qualities have on others is just as important as being aware of those qualities within yourself. For the purposes of this exercise, I asked you to assess how you think others see you. As a follow-up, you may want to check this out with friends and even with potential partners. You can learn a lot by mindfully watching how others react to you. And there's nothing that says you can't outright ask them what they think about you.

WHAT YOU ARE BUYING

We have spent the lion's share of this chapter talking about what you are selling. That should make clear how much I want you to focus on your own self-knowledge. Of course, this should not be to the exclusion of knowing what you are buying. Making good decisions about what you are buying is the essence of the vetting process. Without it, you can end up under the illusion you are dating your dream partner, and not discover until much too late how different the real person you are getting to know is from your ideal.

In the next three chapters, I'm going to help you discern what you are buying. The two main ways you will go about this are:

- Asking a potential partner about his or her past

- Watching how a potential partner acts around and responds to you

In both instances, you will be drawing heavily upon the sherlocking skills you have already begun to learn. If what you have done thus far was Sherlocking 101, get ready for what we can call Sherlocking 2.0!

THE COUPLE BUBBLE

As I described it in *Wired for Love*, a couple bubble is an agreement that puts your relationship before everything else in your life. You do this for your partner, and your partner does the same for you. In doing this, you keep your relationship sacrosanct by holding yourselves within a safe cocoon and protecting yourselves from outside elements. I believe the creation and maintenance of a bubble is perhaps the strongest indication that a relationship will succeed.

You may think that it is premature to think about a couple bubble when you are just getting to know someone. However, I would suggest, this is actually the time you need to begin thinking about it. If you wait until you are completely certain about your future together, it may be too late. A couple bubble does not suddenly appear out of nowhere; it evolves as a new relationship forms.

While you are in the process of learning about your own relationship style and that of your potential partner, talk with each other about your respective ideas and rules for relationships. Find out specifically:

- What makes each of you feel safe and secure?

- What makes each of you feel unsafe and insecure?

- How would each of you handle situations that might threaten your security?

- What guarantees (for example, "I will never leave you," or, "Our relationship will always come first") does each of you want in a relationship?

By doing this, you will lay the groundwork for a successful bubble if you eventually decide this is the right relationship for you. In chapter 11, I describe how you can go about formalizing your agreement to make sure the bubble holds up over time.

DISPELLING MORE MYTHS

In the first chapter, we looked at six common myths about dating and relationships. Before we go on, here are a few more myths, this time related to attachment types and to the process of getting to know your partner in general, that I think are worth taking the time to dispel.

MYTH 7: THE BEST PARTNER IS LOW MAINTENANCE

I bet you think you want to find somebody who is low maintenance. Doesn't everybody want a partner who is low maintenance? I don't know many people who are looking to fall in love with the most difficult person on the planet.

Of course, some people automatically seek out difficult partners. Perhaps it was the norm in your family of origin to take care of difficult people, such as an alcoholic parent or a sibling with bipolar disorder. You think, "I'm used to difficult people, so why not?" And thus, as you begin to date, you are attracted to difficult situations. Or maybe you come from a family in which everybody had to take care of herself or himself. Neediness was not only discouraged, it was regarded as unacceptable. As a result, your definition of low maintenance is skewed. Even a relatively independent person would seem high maintenance to you. To be considered low maintenance, a partner would practically have to be on life support and comatose.

In my view, there is no such thing as a low-maintenance person when it comes to committed, long-term relationships. If your current date appears to be low maintenance, wait half a minute. As soon as you bond with each other, things will change. You will be in each other's care. Your partner's car broke down on the freeway? "Okay my dear, I'm on my way!" Your partner has the flu? "Chicken soup coming right up!" Not to mention, chances are you might end up with that flu yourself within a matter of hours.

So, don't kid yourself by thinking you will find a low-maintenance person. As you will see in the next three chapters, some types of people may appear more low maintenance than others. But none are what I would call truly low maintenance. If you find what you believe to be a truly low-maintenance partner, my guess is it's someone whose unwillingness to take care of you or even to let you take care of him or her will take you straight down the road to divorce.

MYTH 8: OUR LOVE IS THE REAL DEAL, SO IT WON'T FADE

This is a variation of the myth that love is all you need, which we discussed in chapter 1. Now that you know more about the psychobiology of falling in love, we can look at some of the permutations of this myth: for example, the belief—or even the hope—that it is possible to indefinitely extend the honeymoon phase. Sorry, that won't happen.

As we discussed, nature's cocktail is at full potency during courtship. Its chemicals allow you and your partner to be stronger and less passive than you ordinarily might be, as well as more attentive, sensitive, and interested. However, this cocktail has a shelf life. That is a psychobiological fact. The time may vary by couple, but the potency will most certainly fade. When it does, your fantasies about your partner and your relationship will no longer hold you in their sway. They will be replaced by reality.

The fact that the infatuation phase has a limited shelf life does not detract from its value. Without this phase, there probably wouldn't be much buying. It is easier to override your fears or shyness when you have a dose of the right neurochemicals. By the same token, when it comes to forming a long-term relationship, you need a healthy dose of realism. Realism has a very long shelf life.

The good news at this point is that you get to be the person you really are, and your partner gets to be the person he or she really is. We could say the bad news is nature's cruel joke: the person you fell in love with is the same person you later find totally annoying! But don't worry. The ability to accept each other for who you are is what will make your love the real deal.

MYTH 9: IF MY POTENTIAL PARTNER HAS FLAWS, WE CAN FIX THAT

Of course, not everyone is going to be immediately on board with the idea of living with a partner who is annoying. Who wants that, right? It is tempting to think instead of fixing that person. For instance, you think, "I'd like you to still be that cheery, vibrant person I met. Just take it down a notch so it doesn't annoy me." Or the flipside: "I liked it when you were so calm and easygoing. But now it bugs me. Could you take it up a notch? Talk to me more, be more engaging, be more social with my friends. Why can't you do that?"

Either way, this is a recipe for disaster. At the beginning, you find somebody you are sure you want, but then later you feel that person has to change in order for you to still want him or her. Rather than fixing your partner, think of it this way: for better or worse, you and your partner are going to adopt each other. You will adopt each other, whether one or the other of you is an anchor, an island, or a wave. You will take on each other's injuries, past and current, as well as each other's family issues and relationship issues. In short, you are buying yourself a real person. That means to be a good partner, you will have a lot of heavy lifting to do. But so will your partner!

FINAL THOUGHTS

It's in your best interests both to know yourself well and to know well the person with whom you are getting involved. If you can't see yourself clearly and realistically, you will be unable to see a future partner clearly and realistically. It is natural to put one's best foot forward in the early phase of a relationship, and we have already talked about how you can make the best impression when you meet a new date. In addition, you want to be able to look beyond initial appearances and be able to find out who this person really is—not who you want him or her to be, and not who he or she might be trying to appear to be. This requires smart techniques, as well as self-knowledge. The next three chapters, which are focused on the anchor, island, and wave types, respectively, will help you go more deeply into discovery mode. By honing your sherlocking skills and applying them in a friendly and even playful way, you can hasten the dating process and prevent yourself from wasting precious time while getting to know potential partners.

CHAPTER 6

Anchors: Two Are Better than One

In this chapter, I'm going to give you a more complete picture of what an anchor is and help you determine whether you are one. With this knowledge, you will also be able to determine while you are dating whether a potential partner is an anchor. This can be useful, especially if someone is trying to sell himself or herself to you as an anchor when he or she is in fact more of an island or a wave.

I want to say right from the top that the three styles of relationship are not indicators of your emotional health. Your style is simply the natural outcome of your relationship experience. If you identify with one style, that doesn't mean you necessarily have to become something other than what you are. The main point is to understand how you act and react in intimate relationships so you know what you are selling when you begin to date someone.

Relationships can move people either toward or away from secure functioning. The personalities of the two people do not make or break their relationship. Rather, what matters is the degree of willingness on the part of both partners to create and sustain a secure-functioning relationship. If you are an island or a wave, or your partner is either, you likely are inclined to behave in some ways that are not consistent with secure functioning. I suggest you see this as a caution. Knowing what scares you and what motivates you can help you take responsibility for anything you do that might be unfair, unjust, or insensitive to your partner. In other words, this awareness is a good starting point for building a secure relationship.

I also want to be clear that an anchor is not a better person than an island or a wave. Nor does being an anchor guarantee that you will be able to form a secure-functioning relationship. Likewise, dating an anchor does not guarantee that you will be able to do so.

The more I have studied research on attachment styles, the more I have come to believe it's most useful to view your own and your partner's style in terms of "ish-ness," rather than as a full-blooded this or that. In reality, you are most likely anchorish or waveish or island-ish, and so is your partner. Of course, there are always some card-carrying members of each camp in the crowd; by this, I mean people who have been wired as anchors or islands or waves since early child-hood. Many of us, however, have a style that fluctuates throughout our lives. We tend to become more anchorish or islandish or waveish, depending on our primary relationships at any particular time. Knowing the ish-ness of each type helps reinforce the idea that you can choose to move toward secure functioning at any time. In fact, because dating represents a new beginning, it is a good time to do so.

I consider myself to be primarily anchorish. But I also have some island and wave features. I believe I became more anchorish through relationships in my adult life, most notably with my wife, Tracey. Tracey herself is primarily anchorish, having grown up in a family in which she felt secure in her early relationships. As we dated and formed a long-term relationship, our interactions fostered security between us. My professional interest in the application of attach-ment theory played a role, too. We consciously sought to build a relationship along lines that would be secure and lasting. For exam-ple, we agree to be each other's primary go-to people. We always place each other first and maintain a couple bubble. We also agree to be available to each other 24/7 and to tell each other the truth in a timely manner. These and other kinds of agreements have created a foundation of security that has kept our relationship strong.

We begin this chapter with a close examination of your own style. Even if you feel certain that, overall, you aren't an anchor, I encourage you to take the anchor test. Chances are, you are anchor-ish in some ways. From there, we move on to a discussion of the anchorness of your partner and of the ways in which this style of relating can manifest within a relationship.

ARE YOU AN ANCHOR?

Before I define the anchor style of relationship, I'd like you to consider some statements about your own childhood. As you recall, our relationship style has its roots in our earliest relationships. So to know your style, you have to try to remember back to that time, to the kinds of interactions that shaped how you are now.

EXERCISE: THE ANCHOR TEST

Please review the following ten statements about your primary caregiver when you were a child. You may want to have a piece of paper or tablet with you so you can write down your answers. Be honest with yourself because this is for you, not me. Don't rush through the list or listen to television while you're doing it. Take your time and think about each statement.

By *primary caregiver* I mean the main person or persons who parented or took care of you. This could be your mother or father, but it could also be a grandparent, guardian, or other adult. The idea is to focus on whatever relationship(s) had the most influence on you, even if it was not a traditional nuclear family relationship.

I'd like you to come up with at least one distinct memory for each statement before you mark it as true. If you don't have a distinct memory, then mark it as false. Memories such as "he always did this" or "I know he did this because people told me" or "I know this is true because I saw a picture of it" don't count. The memories must be your own and must be specific to you.

When I was a child (before age thirteen)...

1. ...at least one primary caregiver put his or her relationship with me above his or her own needs, performance, or appearance.

   True = 1 False = 2

2. ...at least one primary caregiver would spontaneously hold me, rock me, kiss me, and hug me.

   True = 1 False = 2

3. ...at least one primary caregiver spent a good deal of time with me face to face, eye to eye, and skin to skin.

   True = 1 False = 2

4. ...when I became upset, at least one primary caregiver was able to quickly and effectively calm and soothe me, without dismissing, attacking, ignoring, or punishing me, or buying me off with gifts or treats.

   True = 1 False = 2

5. ...at least one primary caregiver spent special alone time with me.

   True = 1 False = 2

6. ...at least one primary caregiver would read to, sing to, or play with me.

   True = 1 False = 2

7. ...when I got scared at night, at least one primary care-
    giver would come to me or allow me to come to him or
    her for comfort.

    True = 1 False = 2

8. ...when I experienced pain or loss, at least one primary
    caregiver knew about it and attended to my feelings
    promptly and effectively.

    True = 1 False = 2

9. ...at least one primary caregiver saw me accurately and
    knew me deeply.

    True = 1 False = 2

10. ...I saw my primary caregiver as respectful, loving, for-
    giving, and happy in all his or her relationships.

    True = 1 False = 2

Now add up your responses for each of the ten statements,
counting each true response as 1 point and each false one as 2
points.

The highest score you could have on the anchor test is 20 and
the lowest is 10. If you answered true to all the statements, your
score would be 10. If your score is between 10 and 12, it is quite likely
you are an anchor. If it is greater than 12, you are either an island or
a wave.

How did thinking about the statements in the anchor test exercise affect you? Did you have trouble coming up with specific memories? Perhaps one parent was better than the other at providing
security when you were young. Or perhaps both parents were good

in some ways and bad in other ways. Or perhaps your parents did not provide security, but another adult, such as a grandparent, did. Either way, these early relationships have a strong effect on how you approach dating. And likewise for your potential partner.

As you read through the following descriptions of anchor children and adults, continue to reflect on your experience. See if what you read confirms the results you just got on the anchor test.

ANCHORS AS CHILDREN

Anchors generally had childhoods in which the culture of the family put relationships between family members above all other matters. At least one caregiver was fully present and available to the baby. Note this does not mean he or she was necessarily a full-time stay-at-home parent. What is important here is the quality of interaction, not the amount of time spent. The caregiver was someone who was affectionate, and also curious about his or her own mind and thus about the baby's mind. This kind of warmth and interest continued from infancy into childhood, adolescence, and young adulthood.

This attentiveness should not be misconstrued as smothering or engulfing. Anchor families respect dependency and autonomy at the same time. The anchor child is expected neither to be overly independent nor to be overly dependent upon the caregiver. Anchor families operate according to principles of fairness, justice, and sensitivity. Anchor parents have high expectations, but also provide a high level of support so their children can achieve their goals. Nevertheless, loving connection always comes before expectations and performance in anchor families.

Anchor families do not dismiss or ignore or avoid emotions, or fear speaking about them. They do not favor one emotional state over others. An anchor child feels equally accepted when happy and when sad or angry, and thus is secure in the feeling of being loved.

ANCHORS AS ADULTS ·

The secure relationships anchors enjoyed as children give them a foundation as adults that allows them to form satisfying relationships in all areas of their lives. Adult anchors tend to do well in their jobs and to be favored in the world because of their social abilities. They get along well with many people and can tolerate differences. In love relationships, they understand they are in a two-person system that must function as truly mutual to succeed. In this sense, they firmly believe that two is better than one.

I call this style *anchor* because an anchor holds a ship securely in its harbor so it can't float out to sea. In the same way, partners who are anchors have the ability to connect with each other so both feel held and secure. The point is not that they are confined to a particular harbor, but rather that they are able to find safe harbor with each other. When they do venture forth from that place of safety, they still have their anchors, so they can bring their sense of security with them and also know they can always return to their shared harbor.

Anchors are affectionate, emotionally and physically engaging, and unafraid to be themselves. They are afraid of neither abandonment nor engulfment and can easily shift from being alone to interacting and then to being alone again. They are able to define themselves through declarative statements, such as "I choose you." They have the wherewithal to broker win-win situations with their partners and others. Anchors' modesty and humility place them on par with others, rather than below or above. The moral compass of an anchor always points toward mutuality, fairness, justice, and sensitivity. It's not an act, and it's not limited to specific people or things.

Above all, anchors are collaborators. Again, they believe two are better than one. When they speak, they always keep the listener in mind, making it easier for that person to follow them. They do not say too little or too much, or become tangential or misleading or confusing in their storytelling.

Does all this mean an anchor is an angel or perfect human being? It does not. Anchors can be just as annoying and irritating as anybody else. They can make a stupid joke or be late to a meeting or not wear enough deodorant or forget to turn out the lights when they leave a room or a thousand other things. But they are resilient and have a wealth of internal resources. Because they feel tethered to at least one other person, they do not go through life as lone wolves afraid to venture into the world and play with others. Their strength and courage stem from their ability to depend on another. Their secure base was created in childhood and is recreated throughout life. It is what launches their capacity for complexity and self-improvement. Although anchors aren't perfect people, they are free to be themselves, to experiment and explore the unknown, and to tolerate the slings and arrows of life—and of relationships.

DATING AN ANCHOR

Now that you have learned, at least in theory, about the nature of an anchor, let me introduce you to Warren and Sue. They met at a summer youth service camp. As two of five supervising adults, Warren and Sue were in charge of parents and children who were there to donate their time and labor to help build homes for the poor.

Warren and Sue love working with people. Both are hardworking and responsible, and are social, friendly, and skillful communicators. Sue is a tall, attractive firefighter candidate, in her mid-twenties, who comes from hardy stock. Warren, almost ten years her senior, is an ex-marine who has gone back to school to become a teacher.

During the work camp, many of the parents comment on how nice a couple Warren and Sue would make. During their only stretch of free time, toward the end of the week, the two take a short hike together.

100

"So," Sue jokes, "it sounds like everyone has us married already."

Warren lets out a labored laugh as he struggles to keep up with the very fit and energetic Sue. "Yeah," he says. "I feel like they're all my parents."

"Me too. They're such good people. Don't you think?"

"Really good. I'm really impressed. And I'm really impressed with you, by the way."

"With me?" Sue responds with surprise. "Impressed how?"

"By how you handle yourself with some of the more difficult kids. You know who I'm talking about, right?" Warren says, more out of breath than before.

"I think so," she replies. "You aren't so bad yourself. I saw you with those two boys yesterday. I would have lost it. You kept your cool. I admire that."

"I don't know. You're just as good. We're both pretty good at this stuff." Warren stops to look at Sue. "Hey, how come you're in such good shape? Maybe I should train to be a firefighter like you."

"Ah, you're pretty cute as you are," she says with a grin. "I like men kind of pudgy."

"What do you mean pudgy?" Warren snaps back. "Can you do this?" He gets down on the dirt pathway and pulls off a dozen one-arm pushups.

"Wow!" exclaims Sue as she applauds him. Warren gets up and smiles widely, as if to say "beat that," and Sue shakes her head. "I don't know. I'm just a girl." She then drops to the ground and starts alternating arms while doing pushups.

"Go right ahead, girl. Emasculate me. See if I care," Warren teases.

Sue gets up, smiles, and gives Warren a sweet peck on the cheek. "I like you," she says.

"I like you, too," says Warren. "I'll race you back to the camp."

"Wait!" Looking down, Sue says, "Your shoes are untied."

Warren looks down while Sue bolts ahead, giving herself a good head start.

Do you recognize Warren and Sue as anchors? On the face of it, they appear to be. They are socially comfortable and confident with one another. You can glean this from their open, honest, and jovial rapport. Even when competing, they do so in a playful manner. They are supportive of each other, as can be seen from their mutual compliments, as well as their generally positive outlook on life. Neither is threatened by the community's efforts at matchmaking, and both freely admit their attraction to each other. At the same time, they don't indicate any sense of urgency or anxiety about their dating prospects. We get the sense their relationship will develop in its own time, as a result of their shared interests and natural affinity for each other.

How do you tell if your date is an anchor? One strategy is to gather information about your date's early experiences. I'm not suggesting you start to quiz a potential partner about his or her childhood on the first date. That would amount to the over-the-top sherlocking we already talked about avoiding. But during the normal course of conversation as you progress on the dating journey, you can show an interest in the historical aspect of your date's life. The other strategy is to look for clues in your date's behavior and demeanor.

EXERCISE: DETERMINING IF YOUR DATE IS AN ANCHOR, BASED ON HISTORY

Some of the statements from the anchor test can be adapted and used in your conversation with your date, to help you find out about the family culture in his or her childhood home. For example:

1. What was the primary caregiver(s) like as a person?

2. Did the primary caregiver(s) provide safety and security?

3. Did the primary caregiver(s) readily show affection?

4. Did the primary caregiver(s) spend quality time with your date?

5. Did the primary caregiver(s) place your date's needs above his or her own?

You can learn all this with genuine interest. One way to do so is to share information about your own childhood at the same time. You each share your stories. People do this naturally all the time. The only difference in this case is that you have an added awareness about the different styles of relationship that are being revealed.

Also pay attention to how your partner talks about his or her early relationships. Employ your sherlocking skills and see what clues you can glean from your partner's voice, face, eyes, body, movements, and so on. Notice if your partner seems forthcoming with information or is guarded. In the next chapters, we will talk more about why an island or wave may seem guarded. For now, it's enough to know that most anchors will talk fluently about their past.

Let me also remind you that it takes a while to really know someone. In the last chapter, we spoke about one year as a benchmark of sorts. So you need to be cautious about prematurely identifying a potential partner's style of relationship. People can appear to be anchors when you first get to know them, but not fully reveal who they are for some time. Moreover, even someone who is truly an anchor can also have wave or island qualities. This means that in order to relate successfully with such a partner, you have to recognize and take into account those qualities, as well.

EXERCISE: DETERMINING IF YOUR DATE IS AN ANCHOR, BASED ON THE PRESENT

As you are showing interest in your potential partner's past, you can also observe him or her in the present moment, as he or she is with you. Use your sherlocking skills to pay attention to the following:

1. Is my date affectionate with me in appropriate ways and to an appropriate degree?

2. Does my date speak coherently and expressively?

3. Does my date think and act collaboratively?

4. Is my date a good listener?

5. Is my date sensitive to my experience?

6. Does my date get along well with most people?

7. Does my date appear confident?

8. Does my date have a good sense of humor?

9. Does my date ask for my opinion?

10. Does my date seem predominantly happy?

Affirmative answers to all or most of these questions suggest that your date is an anchor.

If you yourself are not an anchor, you may find aspects of this process a bit difficult. For example, if you are an island, you may feel like withdrawing at points if you feel threatened by something your date says. We will discuss this situation in more detail in the next chapter. For now, I encourage you to stick with it. The good news is that if your date turns out to be an anchor, he or she will not be fazed by your reactions. And if your date does not appear to be an anchor, well, you will have learned that, as well.

Remember that the goal is not to date someone who is an anchor. You will be naturally drawn to date people who are familiar to you, and I am not suggesting you do otherwise. Besides, remember that dating an anchor does not guarantee anything. The most it tells you is that your partner is oriented toward a committed relationship. It tells you he or she has the capacity to offer true intimacy, security, and mutuality. Beyond that, it is up to the two of you to build a secure and loving relationship.

IF YOU ARE AN ANCHOR DATING AN ANCHOR

Consider this conversation Warren has with his brother as the two catch up after Warren's return from camp. At one point, his brother says, "It's been a while since you've had a girlfriend. What's up with that, bro?"

"You know me," Warren replies. "No rush."

"I'm just surprised there aren't more women beating down the doors."

Warren laughs. "Friends keep offering to set me up." He describes a recent blind date. "The woman was gorgeous, but still has no idea what she wants to do with her life."

"I'm sure you helped her...and now she wants another date. How will you handle that?"

"No more dates, but we'll stay in touch through mutual friends." Warren gives his brother a sly smile. "I'll tell you about my next date. There was a woman at the youth camp named Sue. You and Mom and Dad are all going to love her!"

As an anchor, you don't need to actively look for other anchors to date. Regardless of a particular partner's style, you bring the inner strength and security needed to be happy in a relationship. Like Warren, you may be good at weeding out people whose styles make them inappropriate partners for you. You just won't find them attractive. So you may end up with another anchor without even planning it.

I purposely described Warren and Sue's initial "unofficial" date, rather than their first real date, because I wanted to make a point about anchors dating anchors. Their secure styles allow for a natural flow as they explore a relationship. Their official dates have the same ease as the scene I described. Of course, simply being anchors does not mean two people are right for one another. It does mean, however, that they have the skills to explore their potential and come to the best conclusion without causing each other undue stress or hurt.

IF YOU ARE AN ANCHOR DATING AN ISLAND

You don't yet know much about islands (or waves), so I will be brief here. In general, anchors dating islands is an easy scenario. As an anchor, you bring security to the relationship. Islands don't want to feel pressured for greater intimacy than they are comfortable with in the moment. You can give them that space simply through your own easygoing nature.

Of course, you may prefer to share more fully with a partner, and this is possible. To build a successful relationship with an island, you need to provide the security your partner needs to heal past wounds and blossom. You will need to be patient. This shouldn't be a problem for you, provided you see qualities in this island partner you believe will attract you over the long term.

The main challenge will be if your partner sticks too rigidly to his or her island ways. If he or she consistently withdraws or isolates as you are attempting to get acquainted, you may lose interest in pursuing this relationship. If lingering past hurts threaten the future as you get serious about the relationship, therapy may help. And if even that does not help, this particular island may not be the best partner for you.

IF YOU ARE AN ANCHOR DATING A WAVE

Dating a wave is a similar situation for you as an anchor. Again, you are the one who brings the security to the relationship, at least initially. You can't count on a wave to do that. A wave's natural tendency is to be of two minds about closeness, so you have to be careful not to feed into that ambivalence.

For example, if your wave date becomes overly worried about whether you are interested in seeing other people, avoid either condoning or condemning your date. Instead, provide straight talk about the realistic prospects for your relationship. Likewise, if your wave date gets angry too readily, let him or her know you aren't afraid of emotions and can handle strong feelings, but also draw appropriate boundaries. These and other dynamics will become clearer as you read the chapters about islands and waves.

FINAL THOUGHTS

Over the last few years, I've received many letters from people who read *Wired for Love* and are lamenting their relationship with either a wave or an island. They complain that their relationship is not as secure as they expect it to be. And they blame their partners. Invariably, these people label themselves anchors. However, their letters also reveal some dead giveaways about their true relationship style. One doesn't need to be much of a sherlock to see that they are not quite the anchors they think they are.

So I want to make sure you understand three things. First, not all anchors will automatically identify themselves as such. Second, there's absolutely nothing wrong with being either an island or a wave yourself or dating an island or a wave. Third, these styles of relationship are not categorical. Being an anchor or an island or a wave is not, for example, like being an Aries, Taurus, or Gemini—born one way or another, and staying that way for life. Being an anchor (or an island or a wave) is a much more fluid condition.

In fact, I would say that if you are unable to find any sign of island or wave in yourself, you are likely to have problems with dating. Why? Because that means you are unaware of some of the ways you respond in a relationship. Either that, or you are aware of some of those ways but have chosen to remain a closeted island or closeted wave because you fear that to do otherwise will lead to rejection by a potential partner. Bottom line: our emphasis here is not on knowing whether you or your partner is an anchor, an island, or a wave, but rather on understanding what a secure-functioning relationship is. Knowing each other's styles is only important to the extent that it helps prepare you to move toward secure functioning (in line with the characteristics outlined in the introduction) and to pick someone who is willing to do the same.

In the next two chapters, we are going to look closely at two styles of relating that represent variations of insecure attachment—that is, styles that reflect some degree of difficulty in becoming close to another person. These two styles—island and wave—appear in some ways to be opposites, but if you look carefully enough, you will see they are really very much alike. For now, as we leave the anchor, keep in mind the qualities this style represents: collaboration; true mutuality; attending to each other's needs; and being fair, just, and sensitive. Regardless of your own dominant style at the moment, your dating process will be most successful if you and your partner strive to incorporate these qualities into your new relationship.

CHAPTER 7

Islands: I Can Do It Myself

Before we get into detail about the island style of relating, you may be wondering how common or rare the various types are. Perhaps, for example, most people are anchors, and identifying as an island will somehow mark you as an outsider or make it harder for you to date. Not so. Researchers have been studying these patterns for several decades, and they generally agree that slightly over half (between 50 and 60 percent) of the adult population identify as anchors, with approximately 25 to 30 percent calling themselves islands and 10 to 20 percent calling themselves waves. Note that I say "calling themselves." In other words, these kinds of studies rely on people's self-reports about their attachment orientation, which makes their findings somewhat unreliable. Nonetheless, I think they give us a pretty good sense of the lay of the land, and clarify that none of these styles can be considered rare.

Much the same is true for children, as Cindy Hazan and Phillip Shaver from the University of Denver reported in 1987. More recently, Sophie Moullin from Princeton University and her colleagues (2014) examined research in the field, including data about the attachment styles of 14,000 U.S. children, and reported that 60 percent had strong emotional bonds with a primary caregiver. This suggests that although your style can change over time, the big-picture percentages for children and adults are quite consistent.

As I mentioned in the last chapter, I consider myself to be primarily anchorish. But I also have an island past and maintain some island traits. When I was a budding young musician, my family was very proud of me, sometimes to a fault. On the one hand, I had an inflated sense of myself as a gifted musician, but on the other hand, I had a deflated sense of self in almost all other things. This family dynamic predisposed me to be an island at that time. The youngest of three kids, I was shy, insecure, awkward, immature, secretive, shame based, and ill prepared to manage the real world of relationship. I was a "good boy" who smiled a lot, acted appropriately in front of family and friends, and played along with what was expected of me. But who was I, and why did I feel so distant, avoidant, fearful, and alone? It took years of reparative relationships of all kinds—with therapists, friends, mentors, and lovers—before I could understand myself and find happiness with a life partner. I'm not saying all islands need therapy to be ready for a relationship—or for that matter, that no anchors ever need it—but my hope is that this book will give you an advantage I didn't have and help you avoid unnecessary heartaches as you begin the dating process.

In this chapter, we will start by looking at what makes someone an island, both in terms of childhood experience and in terms of approach to dating and adult romantic relationships in general. You will have an opportunity to determine if you have an island nature. We will also look at specific examples of how islands relate and respond within the dating context. I will introduce some ways to use your island nature to your advantage while dating. And I will help you identify the island qualities of a potential partner. Once you become familiar with how islands operate, you can apply psychobiological techniques to work with those qualities and not sabotage your future relationship.

ARE YOU AN ISLAND?

As is the case with anchors, it is possible to determine your island nature by considering the quality of your earliest relationships from childhood. Again, do your best to remember back to that time as you respond to the statements in the island test.

EXERCISE: THE ISLAND TEST

Please respond to the following ten statements, as you did with the statements in the anchor test in the previous chapter. Again, mark a statement true only if you recall at least one distinct memory to support it.

When I was a child (before age thirteen)...

1. ...at least one primary caregiver tended to stress the importance of my performance, intelligence, talents, and/or appearance.

    True = 1 False = 2

2. ...at least one primary caregiver discouraged dependency or neediness.

    True = 1 False = 2

3. ...at least one primary caregiver tended to be cold, devaluing, or dismissive.

    True = 1 False = 2

4. ...when I became upset, at least one primary caregiver often gave me money or other material objects in lieu of attention or affection.

    True = 1 False = 2

5. ...at least one primary caregiver tended to withdraw or was aloof, absent, or unavailable.

    True = 1 False = 2

6. ...at least one primary caregiver tended to talk at me, put his or her needs before our relationship, or show intolerance of disagreement or opposition.

True = 1 False = 2

7. ...when I got scared at night, at least one primary caregiver tended to be unresponsive, annoyed, or unavailable.

True = 1 False = 2

8. ...when I experienced pain or loss, at least one primary caregiver tended to ignore, criticize, or dismiss me.

True = 1 False = 2

9. ...at least one primary caregiver often did not seem to understand me.

True = 1 False = 2

10. ...I often saw my primary caregiver treating others outside the family with higher regard than those inside the family.

True = 1 False = 2

Add up your responses for each of the ten statements, counting each true as 1 point and each false as 2 points.

The highest score you could have on the island test is 20 and the lowest is 10. If your score is between 10 and 12, it is quite likely you are an island. Or at least islandish.

═══

It is possible you had trouble coming up with specific memories of absence or neglect. It is natural to want to forget about or minimize negative experiences, especially ones from our early life. For this reason, I suggest you give it some time, and see if any memories resurface as you read the rest of this book, and then retake the island test.

ISLANDS AS CHILDREN

Those raised in an island or even islandish family culture do not receive as much face-to-face, eye-to-eye, and skin-to-skin attention from their primary caregivers as do anchor children. Island caregivers can be less affectionate than are anchor caregivers and spend less continuous, focused, interactive time with their children. Instead of relationships coming first in the island family, appearances and performance are often most valued. Island children do not feel clearly seen and strongly supported by their caregivers. Rather, they feel it is their responsibility to live up to someone else's expectations.

Island caregivers are often more involved in their own lives and not as much in their relationships with their children. They may be overly vulnerable or feel easily ashamed or exposed or humiliated. They may care too much about how others think of them and about gaining approval. Island caregivers tend to restrict emotional expression, either across the board or specifically with respect to joy, sadness, depression, or shame. They may want to acknowledge only positive feelings and may dismiss or derogate negative feelings. If conflict arises, their response is to flee, withdraw, avoid, comply, or, when cornered, attack. As a result of this constellation of tendencies, island caregivers can come across as cold and distant.

Island children catch on quickly and adapt to the family culture. They tend not to be very emotionally expressive, physically affectionate, interpersonally collaborative, or outwardly needy. They accept the island emphasis on independence and autonomy and its unfavorable view of dependency and personal need. Because they play happily alone, they can appear well adjusted. But inside the

113

island child we often find a fragile self that is unsure how to deal with stressful internal thoughts, feelings, and experiences. In terms of attachment security, island children exist too much in their own world, which makes it difficult to bond with others.

ISLANDS AS ADULTS

Islands, like everyone else, wish to find and be in a happy and satisfying romantic relationship. However, they may be unsure about their ability to do so. When they think about dating, they may worry they will once again encounter the kinds of dangers they experienced in childhood or in previous relationships. Before we talk about how to overcome these worries, let's look at some of the strengths of the island nature.

Islands tend to be detail oriented, logical, and rational. Performance is important to them. Their ability to become highly focused on tasks makes them likely to excel at their jobs. They are very good at what they do and may expect to be the best at it. They care about what others think of them, and so they make very good politicians, ambassadors, businesspeople, lawyers, scientists, and engineers. Because appearances tend to be important to islands, they are generally inclined to keep themselves fit and groomed, which makes them good professionals, businesspeople, and performers. They also can be great thinkers and intellectuals because they are prone to spending a lot of their resources on internal processes.

Islands like to be easygoing and not create waves (no pun intended). They loathe spending time mired in personal conflict, and thus are ready to compromise and negotiate in order to have peace. Islands like to think of themselves as low maintenance. I know I said in chapter 5 that there is no such thing as a low-maintenance partner. But islands come the closest. They strive to be as easy as possible. They value their independence and their capacity to problem-solve their way out of trouble. They avoid any appearance of being needy so as not to be burdens on their partners. They are, in fact, the ultimate do-it-yourself people—and sometimes they can get themselves in trouble by trying to do everything themselves.

Many of the islands I have met have ideas about themselves and their childhoods but few actual memories that support their ideas. They tend to view their childhoods as overly positive and dismiss the suggestion of anything negative. This goes along with the island culture of avoiding conflict and of being forward-looking without acknowledging an unclear, conflicted past. The character Don Draper from the television show *Mad Men* and Scarlett O'Hara from the book and movie *Gone With the Wind* are prototypical islands. Painful pasts are easily parlayed into potentially prosperous futures.

Islands are great at handling alone time without feeling lonely or abandoned. If an island's partner is out with friends, no problem; he or she will happily go to a movie alone. In fact, the island may become so busy with his or her own activities that a promise to check in with a partner is forgotten. Due to the cultural demands placed upon the island from early childhood, close relationships tend to be more stressful for islands than for anchors or waves. Close relationships carry too many threats that remain fuzzy and inexplicable to the island mind, so their first experience when away from loved ones isn't loss but relief. From childhood, islands learn to self-soothe and self-stimulate without needing another person. This trait can cause them problems, especially when they're stressed. Their turning to self-care is reflexive and automatic but can be upsetting to a partner who wants or needs to engage. Also, the island tends to experience difficulty when shifting from solo activities to interactive ones but not the other way around.

Islands belong to what I call the *distancing group*. By this I mean that they tend to distance themselves from others when under stress. They find it easier to regulate their own nervous system, for example, when they are not also thinking about what a romantic partner may be experiencing. Their motto is "I can do it myself!" So be careful of overstepping with your island date. Islands are extremely sensitive to feeling trapped by a partner and losing their autonomy. Their history of isolation predisposes them to be mistrusting of partners, and can make them appear selfish or self-centered. They do not feel attracted to potential partners they think might be too clingy or dependent because these behaviors represent what they consider shameful in themselves, and also because a clingy or dependent person is a clear and present danger to their autonomy.

It is tempting to think islands are more independent than they really are. Ironically, despite their aversion to neediness, islands tend to be the neediest of all types. This paradox is often not appreciated by islands or by their partners. Because their sense of independence grew out of familial pressure to be self-reliant, islands can confuse neglect with independence. They aren't in touch with what are actually feelings of abandonment. For example, if your parent always insisted you put yourself to bed as a child, you may have taken that as a sign of your maturity and never registered the loss of opportunity for intimacy. Now, in an adult relationship, you may react negatively to a partner who expects to share bedtime rituals. Unfortunately, islands who have remained unaware of these kinds of abandonment or dependency issues usually cannot resolve them on their own. They require the help of another person. And the most effective person for that job is a romantic partner who can understand the denied, shame-bound desires of the island.

May I speak frankly? If you are an island, much as you may dread some aspects of a committed long-term relationship with one person, your salvation from an existentially alone lifestyle will probably come from a secure-functioning relationship in which your worst fears are *not* realized. For this to happen, however, you may have to allow someone else to be your hero.

DATING AN ISLAND

I'd like to introduce you to a couple, both in their mid-twenties. As you read about their date, see if you can tell which one is an island (or is it both?), and why.

When Jennifer found out that Bradley, whom she met at a friend's party, wanted to go out with her, she was excited. He was handsome and intelligent, but she had no clue he was interested in her until a girlfriend told her and set something up.

Their first date is at a local pub. Bradley is dressed as nicely as he was at the party—which actually was a bit overdressed. Over predinner drinks, Jennifer notices he has a tendency to go on too long about himself and the solar energy system he has invented, and not be curious about her. Additionally, she notices that whenever she leans in, he pulls back. She finds him attractive, but worries some of his mannerisms could be a buzzkill if they keep up.

During a pause in the conversation, Jennifer feels the need to speak up. "Is there something wrong?" she asks.

"I'm sorry?" he replies, caught off guard.

"Is something the matter?" she repeats. "You seem distracted." She carefully avoids saying what she is actually thinking: "Why are you being rude?"

A bit flustered, Bradley replies, "Actually I was wondering when we can order."

Jennifer feels her body tense up. An odd combination of embarrassment and confusion comes over her. Did she mistake his hunger for distractedness? "I must've come off as angry," she thinks. In an attempt to fill the awkward silence, she says, "So, tell me more about yourself."

"No, that's okay. I want to hear about you," he replies.

He seems different now. Not as pleasant. Jennifer worries that she has turned him off. "Okay," she says, and starts to describe her work as a receptionist in a doctor's office. After a few moments,

Bradley's gaze drifts to the couple at the next table. Jennifer's anger gets the best of her and she blurts out, "I'm sorry...am I boring you?" Her jaw feels tight and her face flushed. Why had she imagined this entrepreneur would be interested in what she did for a living?

"I'm listening," Bradley responds, his shoulders rising as he looks straight at her. "Are you saying you need my eyes on you the whole time?"

"Uh of course not," she says with a resigned tone as she glances down at her drink menu. After a few beats, she looks up and says, "I look at you when you're talking, don't I? That's how you know I'm interested."

"One of those, huh?" he replies with a barely audible snort.

"One of those *what*?"

"Nothing," he relents. "Go on—my bad." He looks down at his menu.

The waiter finally comes to their table. "Oh, dear," Jennifer thinks. "We haven't even ordered and I'm already done with this guy."

WHAT WENT WRONG

In chapter 2, I asked you what went wrong in Milo's date with Kathy, and we looked at their interactions from the point of view of the brain and nervous system. Suppose I ask you the same question here: What went wrong? Let's consider this from the point of view of relationship style.

Bradley is exhibiting some island behaviors that are sabotaging his desire for a satisfying dating experience with Jennifer. He's distractible, distancing, and sensitive to criticism. From his perspective, Jennifer is attacking him. Although he wants to make a good impression on her, he feels unable to perform in a way that pleases her. The simple act of glancing around the room affords him a little extra breathing space to ease the stress of getting to know someone new.

Yet, she does not allow him what he unconsciously considers a necessary respite. Although his tendency is to be conciliatory, Bradley feels he has been backed into a corner. Jennifer is signaling that she wants him to approach her closer and more quickly than he finds comfortable. In the stress of the moment, he snaps at her. It is his instinctive means of self-protection, his way of saying "back off!" As soon as he does so, however, he is uncomfortable. He wants to make a good impression, not turn her off. He is caught between his need for enough distance and his desire to get close. He does his best to resume an easygoing posture and smooth things over. But it may be too late for Jennifer.

Jennifer is offended by Bradley's standoffishness. His distancing behavior makes her anxious, and she experiences him as rude, indifferent to her presence, and hostile to her feelings of rejection. We can see from her readiness to confront Bradley that she is probably not an island herself. Moreover—and what is most important here—she does not recognize or understand his island nature. As a result, instead of doing anything to make the situation better, she does everything to make it worse.

As you read the scene, depending on your own wiring, you might have felt annoyed with either partner or both, or you might have identified with either or both. There is no right or wrong answer here. But I think we can agree that both Bradley and Jennifer are justifiably feeling threatened—she in feeling rejected and disrespected, and he in feeling attacked and criticized. In essence, Bradley's island style of relating has thrown a wrench into their first date, and Jennifer's lack of ability to work with his style has only given that wrench a twist.

A DO-OVER DATE: THE ISLAND'S OPTIONS

Suppose you are an island. What could you do if you found yourself in Bradley's shoes to improve this date? (This is not to say that Jennifer couldn't do better herself, but we are looking at things from the island point of view first.)

For starters, you might choose to wear something more casual for the date. You don't want Jennifer to feel uncomfortable because she is underdressed. Consulting with her ahead of time about what people wear at that pub is one small but easy way to communicate that you value mutuality.

When Jennifer asks if anything is wrong, you have the perfect opening to talk about yourself. I don't mean a full confessional. You can keep it light. For example, you might say, "Geesh, I haven't let you get a word in edgewise, have I? I tend to do that when I'm nervous. I'm so sorry."

That would open up the topic of nervousness. Jennifer might say any number of things. But let's suppose she says, "I'm sorry. I didn't realize I was making you nervous."

In that case, you could say, "Oh, you're *not*. I'm just a quiet kind of person, and this is one way I sometimes compensate. Especially when I'm first meeting someone I like. And I like you. I really want to get to know you!" That both tells Jennifer you like her and also gives her an opportunity to say if she gets nervous on dates herself. Either way, it's a win-win.

A discussion about nervousness would also probably preempt the interaction in which Jennifer asks, "Am I boring you?" because she would understand that being distracted by people at the other table is just a symptom of nervousness. But suppose she says it anyway. Instead of becoming defensive, you could take this as an opportunity to reveal something about yourself. You could say, "I'm sorry for seeming distracted. The truth is, I was listening closely to you. Sometimes I don't realize I'm looking away. It seems rude, I know. I wasn't really paying attention to those people. But looking away for a moment allows me to come back and be more fully present with you. Anyway, I'll try not to do that."

This kind of self-disclosure would ease tensions and bring Jennifer and Bradley together. There would be no reason to argue about how either of them handles distractions, and the date could reach a much more positive conclusion.

Am I suggesting you be explicit about your island nature at this point? You could, if you sense your date is interested and open to the idea. Or you might prefer to keep things on the lighter side for the time being. If you are going on more dates, you will have plenty of time to explore your respective styles of relating.

A DO-OVER DATE: THE PARTNER'S OPTIONS

Now consider how Jennifer could tweak her reactions if she is aware she might be relating to an island. Notice also how her responses affect Bradley.

When she sees how nicely Bradley is dressed, she takes the opportunity to comment. "Wow," she says. "You look handsome!"

"Why, thank you," he says.

"I noticed you looked great at the party, too. Do you always dress so nicely?"

"I like to dress well," he replies with a smile.

Jennifer wonders if Bradley's picture-perfect appearance indicates island perfectionism. She knows that while everyone appreciates a compliment, islands thrive on the extra boost to their security. Having made Bradley feel more secure, she thinks it would be safe to inquire into his habits. "Do you ever get a chance to just be casual?" she asks.

"Sure," he says. "When I'm not doing something special." He cracks a shy smile as he reveals something he considers personal. "You might be surprised. I can be a real slob."

Jennifer smiles back. "Glad to hear that. We can be slobs together," she jokes. "I'd live in jeans if I could."

Feeling a high level of comfort, Bradley naturally leans toward Jennifer. "Actually, my work demands that I look professional. I can't remember if I told you, but I'm onto something big in the energy field."

As he continues to talk about his work, Jennifer notices his tendency to go on too long about himself. When an opportune moment arises, she interrupts. Again, she is careful to bolster his sense of security before she pushes in a new direction. "Your work sounds amazing! I love hearing about you. What would you like to know about me?"

"Oh, yes, I'm sorry. I'd love to hear more about you. What do you do?"

Jennifer begins to talk about the doctor's office where she works, and her thoughts about going back to school to study nursing. She notices that whenever she leans in, Bradley pulls back. Instead of letting this make her feel ill at ease, she tells herself this is typical island behavior.

Jennifer decides to try a little experiment. She leans back in her chair and continues talking. She maintains eye contact, with a friendly smile. After a few moments, she notices Bradley begin to lean forward. Despite this move, she remains back in her chair. She is pleased to see that if he doesn't feel she is intruding in his space, he will stop distancing himself from her.

When Jennifer notices Bradley's eyes wandering toward other tables, she feels somewhat annoyed. She recognizes the typical distancing technique of an island and decides to address it head on, but without criticizing Bradley. "What do you think is going on with those people?" she asks, gesturing toward the other table.

Bradley whips his eyes back to Jennifer, suddenly embarrassed that she might have caught him staring at strangers. But she is smiling at him. He instantly relaxes. "I think they're on their first date, like us," he jokes.

"Think they're having as good a time?"

Bradley senses that Jennifer understands where he's coming from. Having grown up in a family where he often felt judged and misunderstood, this is a new experience for him. "Do you get interested in other people, too?" he asks.

"People are really fascinating," she admits. "I get pulled in so easily."

"Sorry if I seemed rude," he says. "Honestly, I heard everything you said. But I know I tend to get a little distracted at times."

"How can I distract you from your distractions?" she says with a grin.

Bradley laughs. "You can start by helping me find the waiter. I'm starving."

"I'm starving, too," she says. "Actually, I can also get distracted. If I do that with you, please let me know."

I think you will agree that this version of the date shows a much greater chance of success. Jennifer does not try in any way to change Bradley's island nature. Nor is there a need for her to explicitly mention styles of relating at this early stage of relationship. Later on, that might be something for the couple to discuss. For now, it is enough for one of the partners to be aware of the island behaviors and to respond in ways that mollify rather than aggravate them, while consistently conveying acceptance, respect, openness, and understanding.

EXERCISE: DETERMINING IF YOUR DATE IS AN ISLAND, BASED ON HISTORY

How do you tell if a potential partner is an island? During the normal course of conversation as you continue to date, you can show an interest in this aspect of his or her life. Some of the statements from the island test can be adapted and used in your conversation. For example:

- Find out about the family culture in your date's childhood home.

- Does your date have only vague memories of childhood?

- Did the primary caregiver(s) stress performance and/or appearance?

- Was at least one primary caregiver aloof or distant?

- Did the primary caregiver(s) discourage neediness?

- Did the most important early relationship seem insecure?

If your date is an island, this conversation may be more difficult than the equivalent conversation with an anchor. Although he or she may be naturally introspective, as an island your date may be sensitive or reticent in speaking about the past, and may in fact have only rather vague memories. As I mentioned in the last chapter, it can be helpful to share information about your own childhood at the same time. Be sure to employ your sherlocking skills to see what clues are revealed from your partner's voice, face, eyes, body, and movements.

Bottom line: pushing or prodding an island will be counterproductive. Best to allow your island date the space to choose when and how to speak about his or her style of relating.

EXERCISE: DETERMINING IF YOUR DATE IS AN ISLAND, BASED ON THE PRESENT

As you are showing interest in your potential partner's past, you can also observe him or her in the present moment, as he or she is with you. Use your sherlocking skills to focus on the following questions. Affirmative answers to all or most of these suggest that your date is an island.

1. Is my date hesitant to be affectionate with me?

2. Is my date hesitant to speak about himself or herself?

3. Does my date appear shy?

4. Does my date often like to do things alone, and never seem to feel lonely?

5. Does my date take good care of himself or herself?

6. Does my date think of his or her needs before mine?

7. Does my date tend to worry or be anxious?

8. Does my date avoid conflicts?

9. Does my date express positive feelings and deny negative ones?

10. Is my date a low-maintenance, do-it-myself person?

IF YOU ARE AN ISLAND DATING AN ISLAND

Two islands can happily create a world in which they give each other plenty of space, yet come together when they wish. To an anchor, this might seem insufficient, but to the islands it can promise to be a very satisfying connection.

A concern when islands date islands is their tendency to be too distant or seemingly difficult to know, to the point that neither individual does enough to create a potentially lasting bond. As a result, the relationship never seems to get off the ground. Commonly, one partner is more islandish than the other. When this occurs, the other partner will want just a *little* more presence, attention, or affection. This can create the illusion that one person is needier than the other, which can cause tension early in a relationship that discourages both partners.

Folie à deux is the psychological term used when two people have cut themselves off from the outside world. Even though they both tend to distance themselves from others, they make an exception for each other. It's as if they form one island. They spend holidays alone together, don't leave the house on weekends, and have no visitors. They create their own joint reality, and ultimately share a psychosis. I'm not saying this is the endgame for all island couples, but it does happen more often than you might think.

For this reason, vetting is especially important when you date another island. Don't isolate yourselves, no matter how perfect that new person seems to you. It's not worth cutting yourself off from family and friends. Also, resist the temptation to think, "My friends and family won't approve anyway, so the two of us will just keep to ourselves." Bad idea. You need to bring in your social network to help you evaluate whether this island can be a good partner for you.

IF YOU ARE AN ISLAND DATING AN ANCHOR

In general, islands find anchors easy to date. As an island, you don't want to feel pressured for greater intimacy than you are ready for in the moment. Anchors will give you that space. They won't stop feeling secure in themselves or worry you don't like them if you are a bit aloof. At the same time, their orientation toward collaboration and mutuality can naturally pull you in and make it easier for you to get close, even relatively early during the dating process. You may feel a bit stretched when you start to date an anchor, but whatever insecurities you bring with you will probably dissipate as you find yourself loved and secure.

IF YOU ARE AN ISLAND DATING A WAVE

Islands and waves can be understood as two sides of the same coin. This will become clearer as you read the next chapter. But for the moment, understand that both types want love, yet both go about it in a manner that is not fully mutual or fully pro-relationship.

At the same time, as an island, your stance of "I can do it myself" is in direct contrast with a wave's "I can't do it without you." If you date a wave, you will face some stiff challenges as a result. Your desire for alone time will be up against your date's need for all-in togetherness. Your tendency to enter more gradually into a commitment will contrast with your date's tendency to rush things. And if you push back against your wave date's insistent need for greater closeness, you will be in for a surprise: he or she is likely to start acting more like an island. Yet a wave's distancing behaviors will be unlike your own, so you may end up simply confused.

Yes, islands can successfully date waves. However, they must appreciate their differences. As an island, you will have to ask carefully for the space you need. At times you may have to sacrifice that space so you can provide your wave partner with more closeness. Your dance together will have to balance your different needs so that both are met.

FINAL THOUGHTS

By now you should have a clear idea about whether you are an island, have some islandish characteristics, or rarely employ this style of relating. Hopefully you also feel more confident about identifying the island traits of a potential partner and feel you have gained a sense of how to relate to that person so you can maximize your chances of success. Above all, you understand that there is nothing wrong with being an island, and that you don't have to change either your own personality or a potential partner's personality.

I'd like to conclude by offering a few basic dos and don'ts for dating an island:

- Do respect an island partner's need for space.

- Don't crowd an island, but feel free to negotiate space.

- Do reassure an island partner that you will always be there for him or her.

- Don't appear overly needy with an island partner.

- Don't appear overly controlling with an island partner.

- Do give constructive feedback to an island, and balance any criticism with praise.

Of course, some of these dos and don'ts apply to all relationship types. For example, anchor partners would also want to negotiate their space and time needs. This is just part of getting along with another person. However, these tips are especially important early in the dating process with a potential island partner, because they allow you to avoid triggering some of the issues that person may carry from the past and help you instead move together toward a loving and secure connection.

CHAPTER 8

Waves: I Can't Do It Without You

Contrary to what you might assume, waves are not the complete opposites of islands. In fact, waves and islands have some important similarities. Like islands, waves come from a culture in which relationships did not come first. Both islands and waves can come to dating with a stance that is pro-self rather than pro-relationship. Both have legitimate claims to having been victims of injustice, unfairness, and insensitivity at the hands of their early caregivers.

As I did in the last chapters, I'm going to use myself as an introductory example. I have already mentioned that although I am primarily an anchor, I have islandish as well as waveish tendencies. The way it worked out for me is that I transitioned from my island phase into anchorship by passing through a wave phase. In other words, I went through a time of experiencing primarily wave feelings, thoughts, and behaviors. (Again, this is not to say that anchors are superior to waves.)

Looking back to my childhood, I see my mother was certainly more waveish than my father, who was decidedly islandish. I say this because my mother was more in touch with her relationship needs than my father was. As you will discover in this chapter, whereas islands tend to be concerned more about losing their independence, waves tend to be more concerned about abandonment. You have already heard me characterize islands as distancing. I characterize waves as clingy. This is the main way in which these two types can be considered opposites of each other.

Today, in my relationship with Tracey, I'm very much in touch with my clingy nature. I love people and I love being in contact with people. When we are traveling together, I hate when Tracey has to fly home earlier than I do because she has to go to work. It's not that I can't be alone; it is just that I deeply feel the loss of connection. Earlier in my life, my neediness was the cause of some suffering. However, I now see it as a good thing—a sign of health, and of having journeyed away from the island ethos.

As a couple therapist, I find it helpful that I can say I am in touch with and appreciate the island within me, the wave within me, and the anchor that I have become. It would be harder to put myself in other people's shoes and help their relationships if I couldn't identify with the different styles. Similarly, I think this is very valuable when it comes to providing guidance for the dating process.

In this chapter, we'll cover everything you need to know about being and dating a wave. As always, take what you read with the proverbial grain of salt and have a good time finding the wave in you. We will start by looking at what makes someone a wave, and you will be able to determine your own wave nature. I will help you identify the wave qualities of a potential partner, as well as how waves interact with the two other relationship styles in a dating setting.

ARE YOU A WAVE?

Once again, you have an opportunity to look into the past and present to see if you can capture the nature of your relationship style. In this case, the focus is on wave characteristics. Try to be as honest as you can as you take the wave test and remember this is for you. Nobody else is going to see this but you.

EXERCISE: THE WAVE TEST

Once again, please review the following ten statements and respond based on what you are able to remember.

When I was a child (before age thirteen)...

1. ...at least one primary caregiver needed my attention or care in order to feel better emotionally.

   True = 1 False = 2

2. ...at least one primary caregiver reversed roles by making me an equal, a confidant, a surrogate spouse, or a witness to matters inappropriate for a child.

   True = 1 False = 2

3. ...at least one primary caregiver sometimes was strongly affectionate, attentive, and tender, but at other times was distracted, preoccupied, and unavailable.

   True = 1 False = 2

4. ...when I became upset, at least one primary caregiver brought the focus onto his or her own emotional state.

   True = 1 False = 2

5. ...at least one primary caregiver tended to be irritable, frequently overwhelmed, preoccupied with injustices, or punishing.

   True = 1 False = 2

6. ...at least one primary caregiver preferred me to remain dependent, available, warm, and sweet.

   True = 1 False = 2

7. ...when I got scared at night, at least one primary care-giver would come to my bed or have me come to his or her bed.

   True = 1 False = 2

8. ...when I experienced pain or loss, at least one primary caregiver tended to overrespond, worry too much, or become overly involved.

   True = 1 False = 2

9. ...at least one primary caregiver often seemed childish.

   True = 1 False = 2

10. ...my primary caregiver expected me to act as an ally against his or her partner.

    True = 1 False = 2

Add up your responses for each of the ten statements, counting each true as 1 point and each false as 2 points.

The highest score you could have on the wave test is 20 and the lowest is 10. If your score is between 10 and 12, it is quite likely you are a wave. Or at least are waveish.

Again, it is possible you had trouble coming up with specific memories—in this case, of your caregiver alternately being available and unavailable, needing you to help him or her emotionally, and rejecting or being overwhelmed by your needs. As adults, we often overlook negative memories or fail to revisit them with our adult frame of reference in order to better understand what they mean for our current life and relationships. You may want to retake the wave test after you have worked with the exercises in this book.

WAVES AS CHILDREN

Whereas island children grow up in a culture that emphasizes independence and autonomy, wave children are encouraged to be more dependent. Wave children have a certain advantage over island children in that they receive more affection, attention, and comforting than do their island counterparts in the first eighteen months. However, although wave caregivers are affectionate and loving, they are not consistently so. Their ability to be emotionally available can be overrun by their own emotional reactivity and strong needs. As a result, they can withdraw their affection and attention. Wave children experience this emotional push-pull as frustrating, punishing, and abandoning. Their response is to cling, feel helpless, be ambivalent about their own dependency, and resent having to wait for the caregiver's warmth and attention to return.

Wave caregivers tend to put too much responsibility on their children to be caregivers themselves. It is not uncommon for wave children to experience a role reversal, whereby the caregiver requires the child to care for him or her. This can occur in various forms: the caregiver may need the child to stay close, need the child to provide emotional comfort, share information with the child that is inappropriate, or need the child to be an ally against another caregiver.

Wave children tend to learn early in life that they have to step up. They feel their best chance of receiving the care they need is to give it to others first. So they aim to please. They can be accommodating and keep up a happy face, because that is what's expected of them. But there's a hitch. Wave children may seem well trained as caregivers, but—like island children, who seem trained to be independent—their perceived strength is also their greatest weakness. They may know how to care for others, but they pay a price in terms of emotional security. They are never fully confident they will receive the care they want from others. Moreover, the continued push-pull they undergo creates an undercurrent of wrath and resentment. Beneath the happy face, there is often an angry one.

133

WAVES AS ADULTS

Like islands, waves come to dating with worries about reencountering the relationship dangers of their childhood. Their primary fear is of being abandoned, punished, or rejected. Unfortunately, this is often what they end up doing to others. Waves can make a potential partner feel abandoned, intimidated, and never good enough. Strange, isn't it, how we can make others feel what we fear the most? But before we consider the challenges of being a wave or relating to one, let's start with some of their strengths.

Waves are focused on meaning and emotion, as opposed to logic, reason, and facts. Their emotional sensitivity can make them great dancers, musicians, poets, artists, theorists, and, of course, therapists. Their language may be filled with hyperbole, reflecting their tendency to see things in terms of "always" or "never," as well as with emotionally laden words and expressions. It can be hard to get a wave to begin a discussion with the most salient points. They like to think out loud and sometimes take time to get to their point. This can frustrate islands to no end. Nevertheless, though islands may complain that waves are inaccurate, the fact is that waves make perfect sense, just not always in a precise or linear manner.

If islands are like cats, waves are more like dogs. Waves love to interact through talk and touch. They want to hold your hand, and always want a hug if you separate for any length of time. They are happiest and most relaxed when they are around people, either in groups or one-on-one. Waves are highly expressive, both verbally and nonverbally. They make more sounds, express more emotions, and just want to be with you. For this reason, I say that waves belong to the *clinging group*. In other words, their tendency, especially under stress, is to run toward rather than away from others. Instead of distancing themselves, they get closer. While the island's motto is "I can do it myself," the wave feels that "I can't do it without you!" Try not to do anything that looks like you are pushing a wave date away.

On the upside in dating and long-term relationships, the clinging aspect of the wave nature means waves enjoy close interaction and loathe the loss of it. It also means they are generous and giving, and have a lot to offer others. Their impulse is to take care of others, even if it means sacrificing their own needs. They make good doctors, social workers, and politicians (because they can see both sides of an issue). At the same time, due to their insecurities, waves can underrate their own capacities and feel they don't have a right to take their place as equals in the career arena.

In relationships, waves can come across as high-maintenance, needy, dependent, overwhelming, and overly emotional. Because their childhood experience encouraged dependency, they may not yet have learned to regulate their own nervous system. Instead they manage their emotional states by interacting with others and taking their cues from others. As a result of this external dependency, they may not be prepared for mutual regulation, whereby partners are safely within each other's care. Their laser focus on relationships can also make them appear intrusive to partners who don't want to be fussed over, talk so much, or delve into the feeling realm.

Because of the wave culture from which they sprang, waves focus their attention outward too much and not enough on themselves. On the one hand, this serves them well, making them highly relational, emotionally available, and interested in the other person. On the other hand, they end up secretly disappointed and resentful that the favor is not being returned. They can anger easily and perseverate or obsess over past injuries to themselves or others. They desperately want love and companionship, but they are not always sure it is worth the risks. Goldie Hawn's character in the 1980 film *Private Benjamin* is a good example of a wave who eventually learns not to look for love in all the wrong places. The *Peanuts* character Charlie Brown can be understood as a wave to Lucy's island.

When I describe waves as clinging, it is important to recognize that their pattern is actually a bit more complex, even paradoxical.

Whereas islands' reflex is to withdraw and push others away, waves alternate between pulling toward and pushing away. In one moment they may cling and in the next they're out the door, or at least threatening to leave. "I can't do it without you" suddenly becomes more like "I can't do it either with you or without you!" Waves can push away a partner through anger, sarcasm, and threats of abandonment. However, the truth is that despite all their pushing away, what they really want is for the partner to move toward them. It's like a test: if I leave, will you care enough to come after me? They want proof that they are wanted and that what they have given will be reciprocated. For this to happen, they need to see a partner move toward them and flood them with positive emotions. Of course, this is often the last thing that comes to a partner's mind when dealing with a wave. Partners often complain that a wave doesn't want them to approach. But the opposite is actually true.

Speaking frankly to waves, I would say that you need to understand that you have been living like a person in waiting. You have been trained to be that way since childhood. However, being perpetually in waiting makes for an ambivalent and angry person. The idea of grabbing what you want and claiming it is anathema to a wave, who feels that wants are either not deserved or not allowed. I imagine waves as locked away in a castle, like a mythological prince or princess. The castle is surrounded by a moat, soldiers, and maybe even a dragon or two. The wave is all dressed up, waiting to be rescued by his or her prince or princess. Finally, one makes it across the moat, dares to best the dragons and soldiers, and breaks down the tower doors...only to hear the potential wave partner say, "Wow, thanks for doing all this. But, you know, I need some time to think about it. I'm not quite sure."

So, waves, this is what I would say. You have so much to bring to a relationship! You are such a people person. However, to be successful in a secure-functioning relationship, you need to deal with the issues you have been carrying since childhood. Perhaps you already

136

have, and if so, that is great! If not, this is the time to begin, before you risk sabotaging a promising new relationship. If someone makes it through your castle door, see if you can take that leap of faith and begin to trust.

DATING A WAVE

Meet Carrie and Evan. As you did in the island chapter, see if you can tell who here is the wave. Remember, it could be one or both of them.

Carrie and Evan met when both worked as nurses in a long-term rehabilitation center. At first they just had coffee several times a week in the break room but didn't date because they were reluctant to mix their social and professional worlds. Recently divorced, Carrie was attracted to Evan's warmth and humor. She pegged him immediately as an emoter, unlike her ex-husband, who never showed much emotion. Evan found Carrie kind and giving. He liked that she had his cup of coffee ready and waiting if she got there before him. He made a point of getting there before her, so he could do the same.

When Evan switched to another facility, they decided to start dating and find out where things could go. Both love hiking and mountain biking and pretty much any outdoor sport. They have gone out for about a month now, and this is their first out-of-town date. We meet them sitting by a kayak they have just beached, having been out on the river all day.

"What's wrong?" asks Evan.

"Nothing."

"Come on," he says. "I can tell something's bugging you. You were all smiles and fun this morning, but for the last hour, you've barely looked at me."

Carrie doesn't say anything. She looks like she is about to cry.

"Hey! Come here!" Evan reaches out to envelop her with a hug, thinking that will help her open up, but she jerks away. "What the—!"

His previously gentle tone turns sharp and he picks up their paddles and starts to walk off.

Seeing that Evan has changed his tone has an immediate effect on Carrie. Instead of sulking, she becomes confrontational. She follows him. "I'm not the one! Why are you putting this on me?"

Evan turns around, confused. He feels like he should know what's wrong, but he honestly doesn't. He feels torn between walking away and trying to sort out the issue. It's their first fight, he tells himself. He'd feel horrible if Carrie walked out on him. Too many people have done that. Not again! So he girds himself and says as calmly as he can, "Okay. Let's figure this out. We were talking about—" As soon as he says that, it dawns on him. "I get it! You're bothered about the motel. You made that sarcastic remark about us having separate rooms. And you got upset when I laughed. You haven't said a word since. That's it, right?"

"Why are you making this my fault?" Carrie lashes out. "You practically admitted you're seeing someone else. And then you blame me for being upset?"

"I admitted? What are you talking about?" Evan feels himself shaking, he's so angry. He has done nothing but try to please Carrie. "That's insane! I'm not seeing anyone."

Carrie stares at him. She wants to believe him, but she can't shake the feeling that something doesn't add up. "Geez, it's not like we didn't already sleep together. And you insisted on separate rooms. I'm not stupid. What am I supposed to think?"

Paddles in hand, Evan starts walking to the rental office. Carrie is at his heels. "You can think what you want," he says over his shoulder. "Apparently you think I'd arrange a romantic getaway for us if I was seeing someone else."

"Romantic? You said... I mean, why two rooms if you really wanted us to be together?"

Evan stops outside the office. "Damn it, I asked you last week about the arrangements. Specifically. You said you'd be more comfortable if we kept up appearances." Before she can respond, he goes inside to return the items.

Carrie sits on the porch. By the time Evan reemerges, she has calmed down. "I didn't mean that," she says apologetically. "I just knew my ex would have a fit. But what are the chances he'd ever find out? Nil. The fact is I was looking forward to being here with you."

Evan pauses for a second, then pushes past her to his car. Carrie follows. He starts the car, without looking over at her in the passenger seat, and heads toward the freeway.

"Wait! Where are you going?" Carrie asks.

"Where do you think?" he replies, fuming. "Home."

"But…"

"But…why spend the night in separate rooms when neither of us wanted that in the first place?" He does his best to sound rational, so his anger won't be so obvious.

Nevertheless, Carrie feels his anger. And she senses there is more behind it than just their current situation. Still, she really likes this man. "So let's stay in one room!" she pleads.

He gives her a quick look. He recalls all her smiles, her many small kindnesses. Was that the same woman who just falsely accused him of cheating on her? "No," he says firmly. "And argue with you all night? I don't think so."

WHAT WENT WRONG

Clearly Carrie and Evan are not having a fun time. Can you spot the wave? Now, can you spot the other wave? Right. Both are waves. Both have been positioned from childhood to feel abandoned, rejected, and punished. As such, both can be abandoning, rejecting, and punishing, as you just saw. Carrie and Evan are both fine, loving people. So what went wrong, and what does this tell us about their relationship styles?

The issue here appears to date back to their earlier conversation at the motel about having separate rooms. As waves, neither was really comfortable with the arrangement. Both wanted to keep the other close. But ambivalence was also present—expressed indirectly in Carrie's worries about her ex and more directly in Evan's laughter. If they had addressed their issues at that point, things probably wouldn't have festered and come to a head later. But that's water under the bridge. In this scene, we might say the first error is Carrie's not responding to Evan's question, "What's wrong?" She signals her bad feelings nonverbally, and then continues to deny she is upset. This puts the onus on Evan to both figure out the problem and fix it. As a result, he feels unfairly pushed away and even punished.

Evan's attempt to comfort Carrie is met by her jerking away. Her tendency to be sarcastic and push away gets her into trouble, even though in her experience, she was the recipient of Evan's rejection. Evan does the right thing by moving toward Carrie, but misinterprets her push away as a real desire to be left alone. Of course, he would experience her reaction as rejecting and angry. Both are waves, so both are hypersensitive to the other's rejection. It's as if they are competing to not be the one rejected first.

If Evan had understood Carrie's worst fears, he could have pursued his attempts at physical affection. That most likely would have done the trick. But since Evan is himself a wave, he reacts instead with anger and punishment to Carrie's rejection. This in turn pulls Carrie toward him with both fear and anger. Her response leads Evan to feel blamed, too, and so we're off to the races. The pair now cling to each other, but in wave style, driven by a mix of fear and anger and hurt.

Eventually, Carrie's tone becomes softer and more conciliatory, but it's too late. Evan is now sunk into his injury and reacts by angrily withdrawing further and punishing her by calling the whole thing off. Interestingly, his attempt to punish Carrie is self-harming in the same way that Carrie's earlier withdrawal ends up hurting her.

As you read the scene, you can appreciate how easy it is for a wave to make mistakes when feeling hurt or scared, especially in a dating situation, where partners are just getting to know one another. You can also see how the other partner can easily make the wave appear unreasonable. However, if you think about what you have learned thus far, and "get your wave on," I think you can understand and even empathize with both Evan and Carrie.

A DO-OVER DATE: THE WAVE'S OPTIONS

Let's start by considering what you could do as a wave if you found yourself in Carrie's position on a date. As you will see, much of the do-over is about holding your emotional reactions in check so you can communicate more directly and thus halt the cycle of fear, rejection, and punishment.

To begin with, I suggest addressing the issue of sleeping arrangements head on. Even before arriving at the motel you could say, "Could we talk about our sleeping arrangements? I'm so happy to be here with you, but this is bringing up some worries. I've been wondering about how serious this relationship could become and whether we are deciding to be exclusive with each other." That gets to the heart of the issue: what is the status of the relationship? Sarcastic remarks about other partners—real or imagined—will always be counterproductive.

But maybe you're not ready to bite off quite so much yet. So you could say something more focused, such as "Can we clarify if we're staying in one room or two? I want to make certain we're both on the same page about that." Actually, anything that puts you in charge of your own anxieties will do the trick so long as you are direct with your partner. Had Carrie done that, the rest of the story might have been moot.

At the beach, there is another opportunity to set things right. Instead of sulking, you could respond to Evan by saying, "I'm sorry. I am still back at the motel when you laughed after I made that sarcastic remark. I really regret that. It was a clumsy way of letting you know I want us to stay in the same room." Or, "When I say something stupid like accusing you of seeing other people, please don't let me get away with it. I tend to want a lot of reassurance from a partner. But I know that's not the way to get it." All of these alternatives are ways of putting your waveness on the table so your date can learn about your style of relationship and work with you to avoid sabotaging your future together.

As a wave, your immediate reaction may be to jerk away from an attempt at physical comforting, as Carrie does. If this happens, repair it immediately. For example, you could say, "I'm sorry. I didn't mean to push you away. What I really want is to be close to you right now." And initiate a hug yourself. Waves (like islands) have reflexes that are self-protective but can also hurt their partner. No worries. Just learn to fix it quickly. This is especially important during early dating because, if left unmanaged and uncorrected, your reflexes can cause a potentially wonderful partner to turn away from the relationship.

Finally, one other pivot point is when Carrie mentions her ex. This is inflammatory and unnecessary, and likely not even what is really upsetting her. You'd be better off saying something like, "I'm sorry. I'm not used to being with another man. It's a bit awkward and scary for me. The fact is I was looking forward to being here with you, and now it seems I've ruined it for both of us. Can you forgive me?"

Can you as a wave salvage this date? Bottom line: you stand a good chance if you make changes early on, before things really go south. In this case, it might seem more difficult because Carrie is dating another wave. Because of his own wave tendencies, at some point, nothing can stop Evan from running away. Nevertheless, the suggestions I provided could turn the date around if implemented before that point.

A DO-OVER DATE: THE PARTNER'S OPTIONS

Let's consider what the partner of a wave can do to help this date without restricting our discussion to double-wave pairings.

Starting with Carrie's sarcastic remark, instead of countering with a laugh or more sarcasm, a better response would be to introduce a more rational perspective. For example, you could say, "Why are you saying it that way? Do you really want separate rooms? I know I have been giving you some mixed messages, but the truth is I was looking forward to being in the same room with you."

More importantly, this would be the time to address Carrie's speculation that Evan is seeing someone else. You could say, "Wait a minute. You just implied I'm dating another woman. I don't know if you really believe that or you're just trying to get a reaction out of me. But you need to know there is no one else. No one. Is that clear?" This could lead to a rational discussion about why Carrie said that—in other words, getting her fears out in the open so they can be allayed.

When noticing Carrie's downward mood, you could say, "You're upset about the motel, aren't you?" Or look into her face with a smile and say, "You shouldn't withdraw like that. It makes me very unhappy. Talk to me. Remember, we're friends. Aren't we?" Or simply, in a playful manner: "Talk to me. Talk to me. Talk to me. I'm not going to stop this until you talk to me."

Being rebuked for offering a hug never feels good. But instead of getting angry, it is more productive to give the other person the benefit of the doubt. A hug may be exactly what your date wants at that moment. Again, keeping it playful, you could say, "So you want to wrestle with me, huh? Come wrestle on the sand and we'll see who wins." But if that type of play is also rejected, you could raise your hands and say, "Okay, raincheck on the hug, but my offer stands. Any kind of hug you want, it's waiting for you."

When a wave date is being reactive, you don't want to make matters worse by being reactive yourself. See if instead you can be a calming force in the situation. I'm not saying you should give your date license to run roughshod over you; ultimately, each person is responsible for his or her own actions. But a little bit of understanding goes a long way. In this case, it is helpful to understand that waves often fail to speak up or take the reins to ensure they get what they want; they are more inclined to merely imply what they want. This can set up a test for the partner. If you want things to work out, you have to pass the test. Now, you may or may not want to pass the test, depending on the potential you sense for a secure-functioning relationship. If you do feel that potential, you can start by providing reassurance and steering the wave toward a more rational means of communication. In this date, Evan could have more likely turned things around if he hadn't been driven by his own waveish fears and reactions.

EXERCISE: DETERMINING IF YOUR DATE IS A WAVE, BASED ON HISTORY

As when determining if your date is an anchor or an island, you are going to listen for wave signs while sherlocking with your potential partner.

Some of the statements from the wave test can be adapted and used in your conversation:

1. Find out about the family culture in your date's childhood home.

2. Does your date seem preoccupied with injustices from childhood?

3. Did the primary caregiver(s) stress the need to be a caretaker, reverse roles, or be dependent?

4. Was at least one primary caregiver alternately emotionally available and unavailable?

5. Did the primary caregiver(s) encourage neediness?

6. Did the most important early relationship seem insecure?

If your partner is a wave, discussing these topics can be frightening and emotional. Whereas an island may hesitate to talk, a wave partner is likely to be more willing to jump in. However, I suggest you tread carefully to avoid opening up old wounds before your relationship is at a point where you are both ready to deal with whatever might be unearthed.

EXERCISE: GETTING TO KNOW YOUR WAVE DATE, BASED ON THE PRESENT

As you are learning about your wave partner's past, use your sherlocking skills to pay attention to the following on a date in the present moment:

1. Is my date very affectionate with me?

2. Is my date often emotional when speaking about himself or herself?

3. Does my date have lots of friends?

4. Does my date always want to be around others and feel lonely when left alone?

5. Does my date take care of others, often before taking care of himself or herself?

6. Does my date get jealous easily?

7. Does my date anger easily?

8. Is my date needy or dependent?

9. Is my date ambivalent, sometimes pulling others close and other times pushing them away?

10. Is my date a high-maintenance, can't-live-without-you person?

IF YOU ARE A WAVE DATING A WAVE

Waves dating other waves is perhaps the most challenging combination. I won't say it can't be done because it can, and I know many happy wave-wave couples. On the upside, these are warm, intense, and all-encompassing relationships. When you date another wave, if all goes well, your need for loving closeness will be strongly reciprocated. You can have a lot of fun together and a rousing social life. However, I strongly recommend you get your wave styles of relating out on the table early on. Failure to do so can cause your relationship to implode before it gets off the ground, as we saw potentially happening with Carrie and Evan. So, waves, surf's up! Get out there and have a good time. But make sure no one drowns.

IF YOU ARE A WAVE DATING AN ANCHOR

As a wave, you will find an anchor easy to date. Your natural tendency is to be of two minds about closeness, but an anchor will not feed that ambivalence. For example, if you get overly worried about whether your anchor date is interested in other people, he or she will neither encourage your clingy or jealous behavior nor condemn it. Instead, you can expect straight talk about the realistic prospects for your relationship. Likewise, if you get angry at anchors, they will respond reasonably. They are not afraid of emotions and can handle strong feelings. However, if you are continually too needy or too unreasonable, and are unable to show a sufficiently playful and cooperative spirit, you may find your anchor date has decided to move on to a more compatible match.

IF YOU ARE A WAVE DATING AN ISLAND

This is a potentially challenging combination. Imagine, for example, either Carrie or Evan dating Bradley from the previous chapter. As a wave, your island date's distancing behavior can be threatening. You want reassurance, but instead you get what feels like a cold shoulder. You want to feel needed, but your island date makes you feel like an afterthought. And when you get angry at your island date as a result, and hope to hash it all out so you can hold on to this new relationship, which you've started to depend on…well, surprise, your island date is already out the door!

In short, as a wave, your insecurities may be fed if you date an island. And you may be rejected if you act too needy. Sound like an impossible match? Not necessarily. Wave and island couples can and do have happy and lasting relationships. The key is to follow the psychobiological principles for successful dating described in these chapters. If you do so, you and your island partner can learn to provide each other the secure foundation you both really want, despite any differences in your styles of relating.

FINAL THOUGHTS

This completes our tour of the three main styles of relating, and of how each can interact with itself or with one of the others on a date. As I have repeatedly tried to convey, it's not about preferring to date one type rather than another. We all have our good points and bad points, and some mesh more easily than others. The important thing is to understand and appreciate the impact your respective styles have as you get to know each other.

Understanding waves—how they came to be waveish and what scares them most—goes a long way toward getting along well with a potential wave partner. Here are a few basic dos and don'ts for dating a wave:

- Do give a wave partner plenty of affection.

- Don't push, or appear to push, a wave away.

- Do reassure a wave partner that you will always be there for him or her.

- Do guide a wave partner to be more rational in approaching relationship issues.

- Don't feed a wave partner's anger or jealousy.

- Do encourage a wave to resolve any emotional ambivalence.

In the next chapter, we'll return to the psychobiological tools you can use to further vet your potential partner. In chapter 4, we considered broadly how verbal and nonverbal clues can help you determine if someone is a good match. Now we are going to assume you have someone you are inclined to feel is a good match, and you want to take the next step and discover more. For example, how do you play together? For that matter, how do you fight together? In general, how do your and your partner's nervous systems interact as you are getting to know one another?

CHAPTER 9

Do Your Nervous Systems Play Well?

Say you have been dating long enough by now to have gotten past the initial jitters, learned something about your dating partner's and your own relationship styles, and begun to think about what the future holds for you both. You may have noticed some of the novelty has worn off, but in its place is the real prospect of a life together. I don't mean that you are finished sherlocking and vetting. That will continue. Even couples in long-term committed relationships use sherlocking skills to better understand their partners, moment to moment. What I am suggesting here is that you are ready to learn some specific ways to improve how you and your partner interact, ways that can help ensure the success of your relationship.

Consider what several couples who have been dating for less than a year—and who feel generally optimistic about the state of their relationship—bring up when they're asked about what is holding them back or putting their future together in doubt.

Ruth and Fabien have increasingly noticed that he wants sex more often than she does. Ruth says, "We don't actually argue about it, but I'm worried this will become a bigger issue as time goes by." Fabien says, "Sometimes it seems like Ruth and I are on different wavelengths."

Jamal and Walter both feel they argue more than they would like. Jamal says, "I think fighting can be the sign of a healthy relationship. I'd be worried if we didn't fight at all. But it seems like we fight about pointless stuff." Walter says he has no argument with that assessment, but adds, "Seems like it's usually Jamal starting the fight. I wish he would be less on edge, more chill when he's with me."

When Arthur and Sophie decided to try living together, they found they have different needs for alone time. Sophie says, "I guess I'm an island. I like a bit of time for myself, especially when I get home, because I'm constantly with people at work." Arthur chimes in, "Well, I'm an island, too! But I've been at my computer all day, so I can't wait to get with Sophie as soon as she's home."

Erica and Faye report arguing about money. Erica says, "We tend to like the same things, but we can't agree on when to spend money on something we like." Faye says, "It seems like Erica wants me to buy her things every time we go out. She thinks I don't get her enough. It shouldn't be all about the money."

Some of these examples echo the most common things we know that couples typically fight about. The Parrotts (2013), for example, boil the list down to what they call the "big five": money, sex, work, parenting, and housework. Tina Tessina (2008) prefers to pare it down to only three: money, sex, and kids. Of course, during the dating phase, kids may not be relevant yet, unless one or both potential partners have kids. However, and more importantly, I don't view the topics themselves as the central concern for your budding relationship. From a psychobiological perspective, I would argue that the concern is less what you fight about and more how well your nervous systems get along.

This should come as good news. Because you may not be confident that you and your partner can overcome the "big five" or "big three," but if you see it instead as a matter of your nervous systems interacting, then you might be able to do something about it. In fact, that is the focus of this chapter. First we'll look in general at how two nervous systems get along, and at some of the common challenges. Then we will talk about what you can do to improve matters. Specifically, you will discover how you and your partner can learn to soothe one another and excite one another, and how you can fight productively.

YOUR PRIMITIVES AND AMBASSADORS AT WORK

You have undoubtedly seen pictures in which people are represented as skeletons. They may be dancing or interacting, possibly related to activities for Halloween or to the Mexican Día de los Muertos. In any case, it's a fairly popular image. I have often thought that the more relevant image is not just seeing the bones, but rather seeing just the nervous systems. Picture two people sitting next to each other, and all you can see are their brains and spinal cords and the full web of their peripheral nerves. I liked this idea so much that I created the image and used it on my first website. I still think it is the most accurate representation of what is happening between two partners.

I know you'd probably like to think of yourself as conscious and in charge of your own mind—and to some degree of course you are. But I think it's useful to consider that, arguably, you are mostly not. And likewise for your partner. When it comes to relationships, acknowledging this can actually get you off the hook a bit. Why? Because most of the time you act and react using the automatic part of your brain—your primitives. Especially when you feel overstressed, threatened, or endangered, your primitives shoot first and ask questions later. This can get you into hot water with your partner—who, naturally, is acting and reacting in the same manner. Your partner suddenly puts you on the spot, and you have to explain why you did or said this or that. Time for your ambassadors to make something up! Quick! But as much as your ambassadors may intend to say the right thing, there is no guarantee they will.

One of the most important things your nervous system regulates is how calm or excited you are in any given moment. Psychologists refer to this range of states as *arousal*, which can be higher or lower.

151

(As I've said before, arousal in this context does not refer to sexual arousal, but rather to your ongoing, overall energy level.)

This is especially relevant in relationships because partners' ability to get along and play well together can be affected by differing levels of arousal. For example, suppose you want to go-go-go all day and evening, but your partner wants to crash right after work. If this occurs occasionally, it won't be an issue, but if it is a consistent pattern, you will need to find a resolution. Levels of arousal also are an important factor when you and your partner are at odds. For example, if your date says something that upsets you, your arousal level will automatically shoot up. And vice versa.

Two complementary parts of the nervous system regulate your arousal level. The *sympathetic* nervous system up-regulates your energy. When you feel excited or threatened, your sympathetic nervous system is what kicks in. The *parasympathetic* nervous system does the opposite; it is what allows you to become calm and relaxed. Notably, both these processes happen automatically. However, the good news is that you can learn to do quite a bit to regulate them.

In general, understanding how the automatic brain works and accepting your own (and your partner's) animal nature can go a long way toward keeping you out of trouble with your love interest. Yes, you will make mistakes despite your best efforts. No communication is completely error free. However, your best chance is to appreciate how the entire process works, and use that knowledge to play well with your partner.

SOOTHING EACH OTHER

In chapter 3, we talked about using mindfulness to regulate your own nervous system so you could counteract the jitters on a date. Hopefully you will have become practiced at that by now. I mentioned at that point that you and your date did not yet know one another well enough to regulate each other's nervous systems. Well, now you do. In fact, learning to soothe each other is one of the most important things you can do for the sake of your new relationship.

As I've mentioned, the part of our brain that is wired for war tends to prevail over the part that is wired for love. In other words, for the sake of survival, the primitives tend to hold sway over the ambassadors. Our brains must register and remember danger so as to avoid or conquer threats to our survival. This not only includes threats in the form of tigers and bears, but also in the form of our closest loved ones. Your partner may not actually be as threatening to your survival as is a tiger, but in your brain, both can register as equally dangerous. Thus, if you want to have a loving and low-stress relationship, it falls upon you to learn to throw the balance in the other direction and figure out how to soothe rather than threaten each other.

Consider June and Wei, who have been dating for a year and have just gotten engaged. Although both are looking forward to a loving future together, the reality is that they sometimes find themselves disconnecting for reasons that neither understands.

For example, when they go to Wei's parents' house for Thanksgiving dinner, June notices that Wei does not include her in the conversation. The family's talk around the table in general focuses on Wei's older brother and his career. Although June and Wei previously vetted each other with their families, this is the first time June has met the older brother. She wants to make a good impression, so she just eats in silence. But inside she is beginning to seethe.

In the car on the way home, she expresses her frustration. "I was looking forward to our first Thanksgiving together, but I felt like an invisible stranger pretty much the entire time. Is it always going to be like this when your family gets together?"

Wei didn't have a great visit himself, but he feels put on the spot by June. His first reaction is to defend his family. He says, "Why do you feel you have to be the center of attention? That's such a turnoff!"

153

June feels her experience is being completely discounted. "That's not fair!" she counters. "I'm not like that at all. You should know that by now. At least I hope so."

Even though Wei has just made the issue all about June, he feels bad because his own issues are not being addressed. "I don't know," he says sulkily. "Maybe we don't know each other as well as we thought."

This is a critical juncture. June and Wei have set each other off, and it is easy to imagine how things could escalate from here. They could have a full-blown argument. Future contact with their families could become strained. If not resolved, this issue could even spell the end of their engagement. In fact, neither Wei nor June intends to act badly and neither wants to damage the relationship. However, due to their respective pasts, their primitives do perceive the other as threatening and act accordingly. In this instance, their nervous systems have been hijacked by their primitives.

I'm not suggesting that if you face a situation like this, either you or your partner needs to go to psychotherapy to fix the problem. From a psychobiological perspective, what matters most is what is happening with your two nervous systems in the moment. Fortunately that is an issue you can do something about, and probably more readily than you may have imagined. Let's consider how.

UNDERSTAND THE CUES

Knowing how to soothe your partner, even early in the dating game, is a matter of understanding threat cues and noticing when arousal is too high or too low. Through practice, you can learn to tell right away if your date's arousal is climbing or sinking just by observing his or her face, voice, and body. In other words, sherlocking once again! Being a sensitive and mindful partner means that you pay close attention and learn the small things that trigger your partner's sense of threat, which then allows you to step in and do something about it.

Let's investigate Wei and June and see what is evident if we pay close attention to their arousal and threat reactions. At the Thanksgiving dinner, June could have noticed that instead of talking in his normally relaxed manner, Wei was talking in short bursts. He would inject a comment with more than usual force, then sit back and say nothing. And when he was silent, instead of eating in a normal manner, his face was flushed and he was bolting down his food. If she'd continued to observe, June would have noticed that Wei's father focused exclusively on his older brother.

At the same time, Wei could have noticed that instead of showing her usually bubbly personality at social events, June was subdued. Her energy level became lower and lower during the meal. Her head was down and her gaze was averted.

Notably, what I am speaking about here does not require knowledge of either individual's history. June does not need to know, for instance, that Wei has a history of feeling inferior to his older brother and neglected by his father in order to take in the present-moment cues about his arousal level. It may help to know these things, but the point here is that it is not essential for the purpose of soothing.

QUICK REPAIR

Perhaps the most essential thing to remember about how to soothe your partner is that speed is of the essence. As soon as you observe cues that suggest an issue, you need to act. Why is this? Because threat is perceived very quickly by your partner's primitives or your own, and threat reactions can escalate fast. Thus, the faster you act to neutralize a threat, the less damage can occur.

Soothing your partner can take different forms, but the two main aspects are nonverbal calming and verbal reassurance. Let's look at some examples.

If June notices Wei's arousal alternately rising and dropping throughout the dinner, she could reach out and take his hand and whisper, "I am so glad I'm dating you and not your brother." She doesn't need to grasp the exact dynamics between the brothers—in fact, that wouldn't be expected in such a short time. The important thing is that she can soothe Wei as soon as she notices his changing energy.

He might brighten at that and turn to her and say, "Really? No one has ever said that before."

If that might seem rude in the context of their gathering, or if she and Wei are not seated next to each other, she could still catch his eye and give him a signal that both recognize as an expression of their closeness. Alternatively, she could find a way to say something loving to him during a lull in the conversation, such as, "Wei, this is such a special time! Thank you for letting me share this with you." Although that might not be fully truthful, it could nonetheless evoke their original intent for the holiday, and she could follow up as soon as possible by going to him (perhaps even while everyone is still at the table) and quickly whispering, "I can't wait till we're alone tonight!" Wei might also want to soothe June in this situation, but the significance of quick repair is that it allows the partner who is feeling most secure in a particular moment to set aside his or her own issues and take care of the other first.

EXERCISE: SOOTHE YOUR PARTNER

In this exercise, find a time when you and your partner can be together undisturbed for at least twenty minutes. You might like to do this at the end of a workday, when one or both of you are a bit frazzled. That's not essential, however; you could do this exercise on a lazy Sunday afternoon as well.

1. Tell your partner that you are going to attempt to soothe him or her. Your partner's job is simply to receive whatever you do.

2. Your job is to experiment and see what has a calming effect on your partner. For example, you might hold your partner and rock him or her. Or you might sit and hold each other's hands and look into each other's eyes. Or you might try stroking your partner's forehead. Be creative. Try a few things.

3. As you are soothing your partner, watch carefully for cues. Notice if his or her arousal level is going down, as you wish it to do. If not, change what you are doing. For example, if your partner squirms when asked to lie on your lap, try to soothe him or her while you're both sitting up. Or if it is clear your partner needs to talk, focus on that rather than just nonverbal soothing.

4. After you have experimented with soothing your partner, ask him or her to tell you what worked and what did not. What was the most soothing thing you did?

5. Switch roles, and have your partner attempt to soothe you. Then discuss what worked for you.

Keep in mind that soothing requires spontaneity. Although the preceding exercise is valuable in that it teaches you about what your partner (and you) finds soothing, and this information can come in handy in the future, we aren't robots. In each situation that arises, you need to be sensitive to what your partner needs in that moment. Watch the cues, and adjust your soothing behavior, as needed.

I mentioned that June might use signals to soothe Wei when the presence of other people limits her ability to communicate more directly with him. In fact, you may find that some of the greatest challenges to your and your partner's arousal levels occur in social situations. Dealing simultaneously with the dynamics of multiple people, not just what is occurring between you and your partner, is often more stressful. This is where the couple bubble comes in handy.

Many couples find that they can manage each other's nervous systems very effectively by developing a private language. This isn't something you are likely to do after only a few dates, but as you get into a more serious relationship and begin to develop a couple bubble, you can come up with techniques for mutual soothing.

EXERCISE: GET YOUR SIGNALS STRAIGHT

Start building your mutually soothing private language by sitting down with your partner in a nonthreatening moment and planning ahead. You might remind your partner of a recent experience when one of you wished you had a way to communicate privately (such as June experienced at the Thanksgiving dinner). Come up with ways you could communicate in a similar future situation that would work for both of you. It could be as simple as a wink, or a few words that mean something special to both of you privately. Have fun with this! It can be as playful as you wish.

QUIET LOVE

A lowered state of arousal is not only vital for health and well-being, including immune system function and digestion, but also for cultivation of quiet love. Creating frequent moments of quiet love will help you and your partner build a successful relationship. Quiet love facilitates the expression of calming and bonding neurochemicals, such as serotonin, oxytocin, and vasopressin. Moments of quiet love include engaging in separate activities while you and your partner are in close proximity, such as both reading books, or quietly enjoying beautiful scenery together.

TAKING RESPONSIBILITY FOR EACH OTHER

Because soothing is such an important skill for a couple's success together, I want to give you one more example of how it can work. This example involves a bit more of a dramatic crisis.

Charlene has dated Keith for only three weeks. She was left at the altar by her ex-fiancé just two months earlier. Keith realized she was not quite ready for a new relationship, but he saw lots of promise in her, so he decided to keep dating her anyway.

One evening when they are out for dinner, Charlene's mood changes enough for Keith to notice. She is agitated and restless, and is not eating with her normal appetite. After observing her for a few minutes, he says, "You don't seem to be quite yourself. Are you feeling okay?"

"I'm sorry," she says. "I don't know why I'm feeling so uneasy. Perhaps we should go."

Keith hazards a guess and asks, "Did you come here with him?"

Charlene starts to cry. She feels stuck between intense grief and guilt for being with someone other than her ex. Aware that they are in a public place, she tries to control her growing panic. But it's not working.

Keith notices she is starting to hyperventilate, a sign of her rapidly rising arousal level. He senses he can help. "Let's get out of here," he says, quickly handling their bill, then guiding her out to his car.

They sit for a moment and he strokes her hand. It is a simple gesture, but he can see it has an immediate soothing effect. As her breathing slowly returns to normal, he says, "I remember how awful I felt after my divorce. I couldn't get over it for a long time. Everyone I went out with felt like an imposter. I kept feeling I was cheating—as if my date was keeping my ex from returning to me. Horrible, just horrible. I couldn't go out with anyone for more than a date or two."

Charlene stops crying. "You went through that?" she asks, somewhat surprised.

"Yeah. I wouldn't wish that on anyone. I'm so sorry." After a pause he says, "Let's get you home."

"No," she says. "That really helped. Thank you." She kisses him and asks if they can go somewhere else.

Now you might be saying to yourself, "My partner should soothe himself or herself. I'm not responsible for his or her emotional state."

In a sense you are correct. In an ideal world, we would all be able to manage our own nervous systems all of the time. But in a relationship, that does not always work. In fact, if you wait around for your partner to self-soothe in every situation, you may wait yourself right out of that relationship. Because your partner may just find soothing somewhere else, with someone else.

One of the hallmarks of a secure-functioning relationship is that partners can depend on each other for mutual regulation of their nervous systems. To do this effectively, you have to be able to set aside your own needs for the moment, and put your partner's needs first. You also have to avoid taking your partner's threat reactions personally. Those reactions were wired into your partner's nervous system long before you met. Instead of aggravating those reactions, you want to be a soothing, healing force in your partner's life.

And beware! If you don't learn to soothe the savage beast that is your partner's primitives, you will get bitten. You cannot train your partner's primitives with aggression, threat, or hostility. You must learn to be a primitive whisperer. In the kennel of love relationships, if you get bitten it's your own fault.

Here are some dos and don'ts for being an expert at calming and soothing your partner:

- Do regard your partner as being in your care. As such, you have a responsibility to learn your partner's areas of vulnerability and know what to do about them.

- Don't give up on learning how to soothe your partner.

- Do pay attention to your errors and fix them without hesitation.

- Do create quiet moments in which you give your partner direct attention.

- Don't make any demands of your own while soothing your partner.

- Do use both verbal and nonverbal means to become a primitive whisperer.

EXCITING EACH OTHER

Exciting love is likely what gets you into a relationship in the first place. As we saw in chapter 2, exciting love is addicting—literally. It employs the same rewarding neuropathways as cocaine and other street drugs. Although nature takes care of love potions in the early stages of dating, it is up to you to create frequent moments of exciting love throughout the life span of your relationship.

It's no secret that partners can become bored and start taking each other for granted at some point during a relationship. Our culture has much to say about how to deal with boredom in love relationship, but little about why it is we become bored. However, the psychobiological perspective can shed light here. Let me explain.

In a nutshell, while your primitives handle the automatic aspects of experience, your ambassadors handle novelty. Your ambassadors require a lot of neurological resources, so the brain seeks to automate new experiences as soon as possible. This is how your brain conserves energy and provides space for new information and experience to be processed. This also means anything new will soon become old.

You are already familiar with how this works. Take the classic example of learning to ride a bike. The first time you get on the bike, you pay attention to everything. After a few tries, however, riding becomes automatic. When you learn to drive a car or learn a new dance, the same thing happens. Or you go to France as a tourist and visit the Eiffel Tower for the first time, and you stand with your mouth agape, taking in the new experience. The next day, you go back and are still in awe. After a few days, you may still find the Eiffel Tower impressive, but you are ready to see something new.

Relationships are no different: what starts out as novel soon becomes automatic. Initially, your new date—this exciting person you've just met—has your brain lit up with activity. Your ambassadors and primitives delight in every detail, and you are on your best behavior. During the first few dates, your ambassadors' need for novelty is gratified and your primitives' need for familiarity is satisfied. But soon your ambassadors begin to hand over this newness to your primitives for automation. You and your partner feel less need to pay attention to your relationship. Why should you? It's comfortable. It's working. It's easy. That's how it is supposed to be, right?

The trouble starts if your ambassadors fully retire and hand over everything to your primitives. Then novelty completely disappears, and you and your partner get categorized as "predictable" in the primitive files of your respective brains. Now you are in danger of making more mistakes because you confuse each other with people from the past. You start to make dangerous assumptions because you've automated each other.

But people are not like bikes, cars, or the Eiffel Tower. Another person is more complex than anything your brain will ever come across. Personally, I think this should make you hopeful about your future love relationship. Why? Because the antidote to the loss of novelty lies in a return to mindful attention. That's right. Your sherlocking skills are not just for dating—they're forever. The way to maintain exciting love is to be fully present with your partner and pay close attention to all his or her quirks and complexities. Secure-functioning couples understand that this is the fuel for a long-term relationship. They understand that they are in each other's care, and that inattention to each other is tantamount to neglect and will only breed boredom, apathy, and antipathy.

So what are you going to do after you have been dating for a few months in order to rekindle exciting love and give your brain that dopamine squirt that makes you want to come back repeatedly? The following three exercises can get you started.

EXERCISE: EYE TO EYE

Perhaps the most powerful way to generate excitement with a partner is through direct eye contact at a close distance. You can do this as an exercise.

1. Sit or lie in close proximity with your partner. You can, for example, be on a sofa or couch, or in bed.

2. Agree ahead of time that you won't use any form of touch while you gaze at one another. You can speak if you wish—for example, to exchange loving and admiring words. But this is not the time to hold any kind of discussion or negotiation!

3. Start with just a few minutes, and be clear that it's okay for either of you to break the gaze if you feel uncomfortable.

Some people find this form of contact *too* exciting and feel they have to avert their gaze. If you or your partner is that way, don't force it. However, many people find that eye contact becomes calming after several moments, so you may wish to at least give it a try.

EXERCISE: MUTUAL ENJOYMENT

Although focusing on your partner is one source of excitement, doing that exclusively can turn into too much of a good thing—sort of like a meal that consists of only dessert. You and your partner want to balance your time alone together with other forms of mutual enjoyment. The idea is to find activities that involve other people, things, or tasks, and that you both enjoy, and make a point of doing them together as a way of generating shared excitement.

You can do this as an exercise.

1. Suggest to your partner that you sit down together and discuss what you might like to do as a couple. For example, you could take a rock climbing class together, photograph sunsets together, join a book club together, or go out to dinner and a movie with friends. Or all of the above.

2. Make it a date. In other words, plan to actually do what you discuss.

3. Afterward, check in with each other. You don't need to have the same set of feelings about an activity for it to create mutual enjoyment. Of course, if it bombed for one of you, you won't want to repeat it. But other than that, focus on how your sharing has brought you closer.

EXERCISE: MUTUAL AMPLIFICATION

What I mean by *mutual amplification* is taking something that excites you as an individual and sharing that with your partner so that you both can be excited over it together. Your joy is amplified by sharing.

And when your partner does the same with you, the amplification that occurs becomes mutual. You can do this exercise even without telling your partner.

1. Next time you are doing something you enjoy doing alone, stop during or afterward and share it with your partner. For example, if you are reading a book, tell your partner about it. If you took an interesting course, invite your partner to sit down with you so you can share something you learned.

2. The key here is how you bring your partner in. Obviously, creating competition between you (for example, "I read a better book than you did" or "Do you know as much as I know?") is less likely to amplify your enjoyment than if you use the sharing to make your partner feel included in your life and loved by you. The basic message you want to convey is "I love being with you, so I want to share this with you."

3. Even if you don't expressly involve your partner in this as an exercise, chances are high that if you generate novelty in this manner, your partner is likely to follow suit and share more with you. Which after all, is the whole idea of mutual amplification.

Here are some dos and don'ts for maintaining excitement in your relationship:

• Do accept that it is natural for novelty to dissipate and automation to appear in its stead.

• Don't accept the notion that you can't rekindle novelty in your relationship.

- Do pay mindful attention to your partner as a way to offset the natural automation process.

- Don't seek out too many activities that keep you and your partner separate.

- Do seek out and create activities you can share with your partner to foster spontaneity and novelty.

- Don't force your own interests on your partner.

- Do communicate "I'm so happy to be with you!" frequently to your partner. And find new ways to demonstrate this.

THE ART OF FIGHTING WITH EACH OTHER

When you start dating, the prospect of your first fight may seem daunting. You may dread it, thinking it spells the end of your relationship. However, I'm here to say that fighting well is an art. If you cannot fight well with your partner, then consider that you may not love well, either. Secure-functioning partners know that fighting and loving can go hand in hand. Fighting should not mean the end of a relationship nor should it lead to threatening the relationship.

In chapter 2, I mentioned oxytocin as one of the neurochemicals that plays a role in the later phases of a relationship. Now is the time to bring it up again. Specifically, research has found oxytocin to be correlated with the longevity of relationships as well as with the ability to be empathetic, trusting, supportive, generous, and communicative. This includes how we fight. Beate Ditzen (2013) and her colleagues in Europe found that couples who sniffed oxytocin during a conflict had better communication than did couples without the extra dose of oxytocin. The effects worked differently in men and women, but the result was the same in terms of their ability to handle conflict.

Don't get the wrong idea. I'm definitely not suggesting you take a squirt of nasal oxytocin if you feel a fight coming on. However, the good news is that you can increase oxytocin naturally. It works both ways. For example, oxytocin increases empathy, but feelings of empathy also trigger the release of oxytocin. Perhaps you can tell where I am going with this. You can stack the deck by intentionally acting in ways that raise oxytocin and increase the likelihood of fighting well.

In fact, some of the exercises you just did, such as the mutual gaze, are very effective ways to raise oxytocin levels. Perhaps you noticed feelings of closeness and trust arising when you did it. The following tips and exercises focus specifically on conflict situations, but are designed to have a similar effect.

LEAD WITH RELIEF

When I discussed soothing your partner earlier in this chapter, I talked about the importance of quick repair—of providing soothing relief to make sure you and your partner's nervous systems play well together. In the case of conflict, this principle applies all the more. Leading with relief during a conflict means acknowledging any injury and diffusing threat as the initial steps in an argument or fight. The idea is to nip a fight in the bud by relaxing your nervous systems so your threat levels are as low as possible. This puts your primitives at ease and allows your ambassadors to come in and take charge.

Tony and Doris, a couple in their late twenties, are moving in together after eight months of dating. Tony went back to school to study art and can't afford a large enough place for both of them, so they decided to move into Doris's condo. This is a challenge for Doris, who has lived there for several years and did a lot to fix it up, as well as for Tony, who is unaccustomed to sharing someone else's place.

"I am so happy you're here," says Doris. "You have impeccable taste, better than mine, and I know you'll want to change some of the artwork on my walls. But can you hold off? I kinda want to keep my stuff up for now."

"Really?" Tony asks as he carries his suitcases inside.

His tone of surprise seems to confirm Doris's worst fears. "Okay," she says, "so you think my taste in art really sucks?"

"No, no!" Tony puts down his bags and goes over to Doris. "I'm sorry. I know I'm an art snob. I admit it. In most cases, I like what you like. It's just that art is my business, you know? I sell the stuff. But I'm not coming to live with your art; I'm coming because I love you. You are adorable. I won't change a thing… For now. But down the line, maybe…" He squints and tilts his head, so Doris gets what he is thinking.

"Fine," she says. "But I want to be part of the choice process. Okay?"

"Absolutely."

In this example, Tony effectively led with relief. He immediately saw that Doris was reacting out of threat, and he was able to soothe and reassure her. At the same time, he let her know that they would continue to work on this issue in the future in a nonthreatening manner.

The following are the kinds of statements you can use to lead with relief in an interaction that appears to be leading to conflict:

- "I'm sorry. I didn't realize you felt that way."

- "I guess you're right; I am jealous."

- "I felt really hurt when you said that."

- "I know this is something we both feel strongly about, but let's see if we can talk it out."

- "I want you to be able to tell me what you feel, whatever you feel, without worrying that I can't handle it."

- "Can we sit quietly before we discuss this? If we do some mindful breathing together, I think it will be easier to talk about the hard stuff."

- "Come here and give me a hug. Even if we aren't seeing eye to eye right now, you know how much I love you, don't you?"

- "We were really talking past each other earlier. Before we get into any of the details, I want to make sure we're still good. Yes?"

Statements such as these provide reassurance and literally allow the nervous system to relax. Moreover, this trains the automatic brain to remember this experience for the next time. When tensions arise in the future, your primitives are less likely to go into survival mode and react with high alert because they aren't so scared of losing a battle or failing to get what they think you need and want.

EXERCISE: PUT YOURSELF IN YOUR PARTNER'S SHOES

To get what you want, you have to ensure that your partner gets what he or she wants. Top negotiators understand this. They study their opposition well to know their fears, hopes, and desires. And they often lead with this knowledge so as to relax the other party. You don't have to be an expert negotiator to fight well and get what you want with your partner. But you do have to think in terms of mutuality, collaboration, and concern for your partner's interests.

This exercise is purposely designed for a situation that falls short of outright fighting, although making decisions can and does lead to fights.

1. Next time you and your partner are deciding where to go on a date, and you've each come up with different first choices (e.g., you want one restaurant or movie, and your partner wants a different restaurant or movie), stop for a moment.

169

Ask your partner what he or she really likes best about his or her choice. Listen to what your partner says.

2. Now put yourself in your partner's shoes. If your partner wants to go to a particular restaurant because it has the world's best salad dressing, can you empathize with that?

3. Consider whether your understanding and empathy for your partner's choice are strong enough to let go of your own opposing choice, at least for this one date. If it is, your decision is made!

Putting yourself in your partner's shoes doesn't mean you should always put his or her choices before your own, or become a doormat. Not at all. Remember, you are aiming for mutuality. However, it does mean that you need to develop the willingness to put your partner's needs before your own at least some of the time. Hence the value of this exercise in discovering and experimenting with what it feels like to lead with empathy.

CO-REGULATE CONFLICT PLAYFULLY

Secure-functioning partners are playful. Their play zone is large enough to include conflict-filled interactions. And, yes it's quite possible to fight and be playful at the same time. It's similar to the kind of play you hopefully enjoyed with at least one of your parents as a child. Stephen Porges (2009), a leader in arousal regulation research, points out that mammals engaged in rough-and-tumble play maintain eye contact. He gives the example of playing with a dog. If you have ever accidently stepped on or hurt a dog, you may have noticed that the dog immediately seeks reassurance by looking at you. In other words, the dog does not assume the worst; rather, it makes a point of establishing—and if necessary, reestablishing—trust so no actions fall outside the play zone. And it does this through visual contact.

And so it is with humans. If you are going to fight with your partner, make sure you are in relatively close proximity so your near visual systems are engaged. As we discussed in chapter 2, the brain's threat reaction system becomes more activated when you see faces at a glance or to the side. In large part, this has to do with the mechanics of the eye. The macula contains the fovea, an area the size of a pinhead, which sees the world in high definition. Outside that area, we are legally blind. The illusion that we can see clearly outside that area is provided through rapid eye movement. Thus, if you are talking about important matters while driving in a car or walking side by side, you become more vulnerable to mistaken threat cues. Communicating solely by phone, or worse yet by email or text messaging, only increases the possible mistakes your primitives and ambassadors can make. Of course, talking while driving or walking side by side or on the phone or through texting is not a problem when you are feeling good. But if you and your partner start to feel bad and need to regulate one another's nervous systems, then not having direct eye contact becomes a huge disadvantage and can exacerbate fights.

After living together for several weeks, Doris has become angry that Tony throws his clothes around and doesn't pick up after himself. A few reminders have not done the trick, and she's beginning to feel resentful.

"Okay, handsome man," she begins. "You're not getting away with your slobbery." She leans against the doorjamb, arms folded, head cocked, and winks at Tony, who has just walked in.

He lets out a sigh as he drops his jacket on the floor. "You mean this kind of slobbery?"

"Yeah."

"Isn't that what you're here for?" he says, giving her an evil smile.

"Come here for your beating," says Doris, beckoning with her index finger. "But before you do, pick up that jacket."

"Anything for you," replies Tony as he picks up his jacket and gives her a kiss.

"Now look in my eyes and tell me you will pick up your stuff." Doris has Tony by his collar. "If you don't, I'm going to have to train you like the cute dog you are."

"Deal. I don't mind being trained by you. But will you do one thing for me?"

"Anything."

"I love your sense of humor and I love you, but when I enter the room, could you greet me with something nice...and then tell me what I've done wrong?"

"I'm sorry," she says. "I can do that. I guess I was starting to feel angry, and I didn't want that to carry through the night."

Tony kisses her. "I appreciate that. And I do want you to tell me things that bother you. Just not the very first thing when I walk in. The second thing is fine."

You may say that Tony and Doris are being overly sweet. Since they are in a new relationship, it's natural for them to be a bit cautious. But that shouldn't take away from this example of how a couple can get their points across and influence the other without using fear or threat or guilt. Tony and Doris seem well on their way to a successful relationship through their ability to lead with relief, empathize and show appreciation for the other, and get what each needs without going to war.

Here are some dos and don'ts for fighting well with your partner:

- Do make sure you are in close visual proximity to your partner when entering into conflict.

- Don't position yourself to the side of your partner, but make sure you are straight on, face to face and eye to eye.

- Don't manage conflict over the phone or via email or text messaging.

- Don't focus only on your own concerns, needs, and wants; know your partner's needs and wants and concerns and be able to articulate them.

- Do always lead with relief. Explain, justify, or counter only when relief has been achieved.

- Don't assume that your partner knows you are being friendly and not threatening.

- Do use your ambassadors to come up with mutually agreeable solutions. Use your primitives to feel and empathize.

- Don't act as if you are the only person (or the most important person) in the relationship.

FINAL THOUGHTS

If you were looking to this chapter for ways to prevent you and your partner from ever fighting, or even for better ways to win an argument, you must have figured out by now that I'm not offering that. Of course, much more could be said about how you and your partner can negotiate your differences and disagreements. An entire book could be written about that. But I have another focus here: I want you to understand and appreciate the crucial role of your respective nervous systems in how well you get along with each other over the long term. If you can build on what you learned in the earlier chapters about calming yourself, and now add to that the ability to mutually calm and attune with your partner, I believe you have the most powerful tools to stack the odds in your favor.

CHAPTER 10

Breaking Up

"You're never gonna change!" cries Angel as she strides out of the one-bedroom apartment she has recently begun sharing with Mickey, her boyfriend of nine months.

"Come on, not *again*!" Mickey follows her to the door, his voice a mix of defeated and hopeful. "I know I can be frustrating. But that doesn't mean I don't love you, baby. Please, just calm down and give me some space to breathe. Not everything can go at the speed you want. I mean, look! We're in our new place. This is far more than I've done before, right?"

"It's too little for too much work and arguing," says Angel. "I don't think you get it. Either you don't understand women, or you don't understand me, or you're just a total moron. We talk about getting married. You tease me with dates and then don't follow through. You play around at work so much that, I don't know, maybe you actually want to get fired. We talk about kids and you're all excited, but then it's like we never said anything. It's crazy making! You have to grow up, Mickey. My mom says I'm wasting the best years of my life. I love you so much, but where's our future? I'm not going to do this to myself anymore. I can't."

Mickey becomes quiet, head down, nursing the beer left in his bottle. "Okay. So you're leaving me?"

Angel's tone changes. She looks at Mickey and says in a somber voice, "I'm so sorry. I know I've done this twice already. But this time I mean it. I deserve more. And you don't need a woman nagging you all the time. I'm moving out tonight. My mom and brother will be helping carry stuff, so I don't think you'll want to be here, since you don't get along with either of them." She pauses, then closes the door. From inside, Mickey can hear her say, "I'm sorry."

Despite your best efforts to launch a secure-functioning, long-term relationship, you may not succeed. Unfortunately, there are no guarantees in this business. I can give you all the tools to stack the odds in your favor, but that still does not mean that every potential partner will be the right one for you. Because I'm aware of this, I have included a full chapter on breaking up.

Just as there are more effective and less effective ways to approach dating, there are also more and less effective ways to conduct a breakup. Much of what you have learned in the previous chapters applies to the ending of a relationship. Hopefully you already got a sense of that from reading the brief example of Angel and Mickey. Based on what you know, you probably recognized some of the reasons this couple did not last. For example, Angel mentions the animosity between Mickey and her family, suggesting that either this couple did not properly vet each other—or at least one of them did not listen to and follow the vetting advice.

In this chapter, we discuss the reasons you should end or consider ending a relationship, and how best to go about a breakup when you decide it is the best course of action. Sometimes couples come to a mutual decision to end their relationship. (Ironically, some of those couples may be the ones least in need of ending their relationship.) More often, one or another partner leads the charge. So here we look at what to do when your partner may not want to call it quits, as well as how to handle things when your partner is the main one pushing a breakup.

WHY SOME RELATIONSHIPS DON'T LAST

As we examine the reasons some relationships don't last, I'd like to start with the caveat that when relationships fail, it is rarely just one person's fault.

"How can that be?" you ask. "Doesn't failure imply fault?"

The answer depends upon how you think about fault. From a psychobiological perspective, we see that people are incredibly complex, and relationships even more so. There are two people, two brains, two nervous systems, and two family histories involved in any love relationship. Thus, neither partner is in complete control of the outcome. Likewise, neither is likely to be the only one at fault. Moreover, casting blame—as we shall see—will not save a failing relationship.

So ease up on yourself. Don't be discouraged if your relationship ends. The important thing is that you are doing your best. And you are learning to do better and be better. The purpose of this book is to guide you to find not just any partner, but a partner with whom you can have a secure-functioning relationship based on true mutuality, justice, fairness, and sensitivity. Have patience, and give yourself enough time.

I think it is helpful to consider some of the main reasons that relationships fail. If you refer back to the introductory chapter, where I list the five characteristics of a secure-functioning relationship, you will find a direct correspondence between those characteristics and these reasons for failure. In short, relationships are most likely to fail if the partners don't follow the principle of secure functioning.

Reason 1. At least one partner maintains one foot in and one foot out of the relationship.

On the surface, this is a reflection of the inability to commit. In Angel's case, she complained about Mickey's empty promises and his lack of follow-through after dates. But it also goes deeper than the hesitancy to commit: having one foot in and one foot out of a dating relationship creates an underlying feeling of insecurity. Instead of feeling protected, the other partner feels unsafe. You might think this could work as long as both partners maintain this stance. While that might be true for a while, I wouldn't put my bets on that kind of arrangement leading to anything lasting. And even if for some reason it does manage to last, it still would not be considered a secure-functioning relationship.

Reason 2. Either partner is strongly an island or a wave, or both are.

While I have stated that the various kinds of island/wave combinations can be successful, I have also made it clear that these relationships generally have more hurdles to get over than do two anchors. In our example, Angel and Mickey appear to be a wave and an island, respectively. Is that the sole cause of their breakup? Definitely not. But does it play a role? Yes, especially if they are strongly islandish or waveish. Issues of justness, fairness, and sensitivity can mount up, and unless the partners learn how to appreciate and work with each other's different styles, they are unlikely to make it together over the long run.

Reason 3. Partners do not notice or repair injuries.

Good relationships don't stem from perfect behavior, but rather from being willing to admit mistakes and make amends. It's all about repair. And this needs to begin, as we saw in the last chapter, during dating. Some people have such a long history of pain and hurt that they run roughshod over their partners and expect to get away with it. Others don't notice the injuries they cause others. It may look like they simply don't care, but some people actually are unable to tell if their partners are happy. Perhaps the most common cause of breakups is the inability to notice and respond to injuries posthaste.

Reason 4. Partners are not good, as a team, at regulating each other's internal states.

This is as true for creating mutual excitement as it is for reducing mutual distress. Partners who are unable to do this are like a time bomb. They can only go on for so long in the addictive phase of new love, which runs on dopamine. Unless they learn to create a quieter, more stable kind of love that runs on serotonin, the excitement they may feel will not be balanced by comfort and relaxation. As soon as they try to face the usual stresses of daily life together, they are likely to implode. They may even appear as predators to one another. They never meant for this to happen, but they didn't have the skills to do better. Threat management is a huge part of a successful long-term relationship. Partners' inability to regulate each other is a strong predictor of relationship breakup.

Reason 5. Partners don't get the importance of primacy.

Those who come from a family in which relationships came first—above appearances, performance, caretaking, or anything else—are at a distinct advantage during the dating process. They understand the need to protect the primacy of their bond against anything or anyone who might be seen as competing with it. This competition comes from what I call "thirds," which include other people (for example, kids, in-laws, ex-partners), jobs, tasks, hobbies, drugs and alcohol, pornography, and more. Of course, thirds can interact with the couple system, as long as the partners understand their relationship always comes first. During initial dating, this may not seem as important, but for a relationship to go further, it becomes crucial.

Reason 6. There is no couple bubble.

If they have been dating for a while, partners should have been able to create a couple bubble. This bubble is based on the recognition of primacy. It also manifests the other characteristics of secure functioning that I have just been discussing (such as security and the quick repair of injuries). If there is anything that comes close to providing insurance that a relationship will last, it is the couple bubble. A bubble may take time to create and strengthen, but until that happens, a relationship is vulnerable to failure.

SHOULD YOU SAY GOOD-BYE?

The decision to end a relationship is not something you want to do lightly. Let's assume you made it through some months (or even a year) of dating and seriously engaged in the vetting process—introducing your potential partner to family and friends, plus sherlocking carefully yourself. At this point, you probably feel you have a lot invested. If things are going really well, fantastic! You are ready to take your relationship to the next level. The next chapter is all about how you can do that. However, you may instead be feeling one of two ways: certain you no longer want to pursue this relationship, or uncertain whether or not it is time to call it quits.

If the latter case describes you, here is a list of questions to ask yourself. To be clear, no one should decide to end a relationship solely based on a questionnaire in a book. Nevertheless, I think you will see that these questions don't arise out of thin air. They closely relate to everything that has been covered here thus far. So please consider these questions within the context of everything you have been reading and learning about, and let them inform your decision accordingly.

1. Do you or this partner have one foot in and one foot out of the relationship?

2. Is it hard for you or this partner to feel relaxed and comfortable around the other?

3. Is it hard for you or this partner to feel safe and secure around the other?

4. Has any abuse or violence occurred in this relationship?

5. Do you or this partner resist having sex with the other?

6. Are you or this partner strongly an island or a wave?

7. Do you find it hard to tell how this partner is feeling?

8. Does this partner show little or no interest in your feelings?

9. Do you or this partner find it hard to calm or soothe the other?

10. Do you or this partner ever let thirds (such as people or tasks) take precedence over the relationship? (Note: This could include cheating or betrayal, but it doesn't have to get that far.)

11. If you or this partner feels hurt or injury, does the other fail to repair it right away?

12. Have you and this partner tried to talk over your differences, but failed?

13. Do you and this partner fight frequently, nastily, or without resolution? (Note: The question is not whether you fight at all.)

14. Have you or this partner already tried on one or more occasions to break up?

15. Do you and this partner keep secrets from each other?

16. Do you have no sense of future with this partner?

17. Did vetting with either your or this partner's family and friends yield negative results?

18. Would you say a couple bubble has not even begun to form for you and this partner?

I purposely made this a lengthy list because, to be honest, if your answer to every question here is yes, you have very, very, very strong grounds for ending this relationship. I'm not going to give you a formula to calculate exactly how many yeses you need before you should arrive at that conclusion. What you see as a deal breaker may not be the same as someone else's deal breaker. If abuse or any form of violence exists in the relationship, you should end it immediately. Beyond that, the more yeses you have to these questions, the more shaky the ground you are on and the more seriously you should consider whether dating someone else would be a better option at this point.

HOW TO SAY GOOD-BYE

Saying good-bye is never easy. Even if you are 100 percent certain you want out of a relationship, actually saying so to your partner and making it happen can be hard, especially if your partner disagrees or is upset. In fact, the principle of secure functioning applies not just to your dating relationship, but also to how you approach a breakup. This may sound like a contradiction in terms, but let's see how it can work.

The following is a conversation between two partners who (unlike Angel and Mickey in our earlier example) are basically on the same page about breaking up. They may not want to break up and may have strong feelings of distress about it, but they are nevertheless in agreement about what should happen. It could be an anchor couple, but not necessarily. The important thing is that they act mindfully and observe the kind of sensitivity, fairness, and mutuality characteristic of secure functioning even when they are jointly involved in ending their relationship.

Meet Drew and George, who have been dating for almost a year. They are both in their forties; Drew had recently ended a ten-year relationship, while George had serial relationships as well as significant stretches of being single. They found each other online and quickly became exclusive. Now they are sitting in George's living room on a Saturday morning, having just finished breakfast together, which Drew cooked.

Drew: I know neither of us has been wanting to have this conversation. But I also know, and I think you do too, that we need to do it.

George: Yes, I know what you're going to say. And yeah, I'm feeling that way, too.

Drew: (*breathes once, mindfully, and holds eye contact with George*) First, I want you to realize how much our time together has meant to me. I wouldn't trade it for the world! You're such a genuine, warm-hearted, fun-to-be-with person. Traveling together has been some of the best time of my life. And also just the quiet times, like this morning. (*pauses*) At the same time, well... I have to admit, it just isn't working.

George: (*tearing up*) It's really hard to face this. I'm glad you brought it up because, quite honestly, I don't think I could've done it.

Drew: It's tough. Especially considering how much we both tried to make this work.

George: (*rallying*) But what does it really come down to for you? I mean, why can't we just give it one more try?

Drew: (*shakes head*) I know—I'm as frustrated as you are. But I don't think that would make a difference. And I don't think it's good for either of us to prolong this.

George: I suppose you're right...

Drew: Let me try to put into words what I'm experiencing. I want us both to be clear that I don't see this as a matter of blame. For me, it's just that I feel alone a lot of the time. You're off painting in your studio, and I don't seem to have that ability to occupy myself like that. I'm more like a needy little kid.

George: I know I have a tendency to go off into my own world, and I don't keep in contact. I'm sorry about that. It has nothing to do with how much I care about you. It's just how I operate inside.

Drew: I know. And that's the thing: it's how you are, and I don't want to change that about you. I respect your artwork. If anything, I wish I had something like that myself.

George: Yeah. And we really have tried to make that work. But it just keeps coming up wrong.

Drew: And it's not that I think you're ignoring me, or love me any less, or are ever going to cheat on me. I know you're not. It's just that I have different needs than you do in a relationship. I need a lot more close, shared personal time. Like the kind of closeness we'd have if we went into business together or something. Except that's not something we're about to do.

George: You know, we hardly ever fight. Not like in other relationships I've had.

Drew: Sometimes I think it would be better if we fought more. I mean, the fights we do have tend to be about petty issues. It's like we don't know how to fight about the big stuff.

George: I really have no big issues I want to fight about with you.

Drew: *(laughs)* Well, I guess I don't, either.

George: So it comes down to a basic difference in what we need. I can't disagree with any of this.

Drew: I'm going to be traveling for my job over the next month. That will make the transition easier for both of us.

George: So you mean…this is it?

Drew: *(sighs)* I think a clean break will be easier on both of us. Don't you?

George: I guess. But can't we stay friends?

Drew: I'm not sure how I feel about that right now. Why don't we give it some time. I'd like to check in with you after I'm back in town, see how you're doing—see how we're both doing. We can see what feels right at that point.

So, I think you can see that Drew and George treat one another with respect as well as do their best to regulate their own and each other's nervous systems as they talk. You may be thinking, "If their relationship is so bad that they have to break up, how can you expect them to act so positively?" From my perspective, it doesn't matter whether you are on a date, breaking up, or celebrating your fiftieth wedding anniversary—every moment is an opportunity to move closer to secure functioning. It's all a learning process. And as such, whatever you learn now you can carry into your next relationship to increase your chance of success.

Here are some guidelines you can apply to most breakup scenarios:

- Talk to your partner in person.

- Meet in a quiet and safe location, one that feels neutral to you both.

- Scan your body regularly for tensions that arise, and let them go.

- Express the positives about your relationship, not just the negatives.

- Be clear about your reasons for breaking up.

- Hear each other out.

- Stick to your decision.

- Clarify any logistics related to going your separate ways.

If you are initiating a breakup with someone who either wants the relationship to continue or is too angry to know if he or she wants to be in or out of the relationship, your task is more difficult. You can still aim for the secure-functioning model, but adjust accordingly. For example, if your partner gets too argumentative or becomes belligerent, you may need to cut the discussion short. As always, if abuse or violence (or even the threat thereof) is present, disengage immediately.

How to Take a Good-Bye

Truly speaking, if your partner initiates and insists upon a breakup that you don't really want, the best way to take the news is to aim for the mindful, secure-functioning model we've just been discussing. A secure-functioning relationship is all about mutuality, so you won't gain anything by pushing back against a breakup. Trying to convince someone to date you if that person does not want to is never going to work. So, go ahead and discuss the situation, listen to what your partner has to say, and share your feelings, but do so in a mindful, considerate, and caring way. At the same time, recognize that no matter how high your hopes were for this relationship to work out, there are many other fish in the sea.

FINAL THOUGHTS

Beyond the breakup conversation, take some time for yourself. This applies whether the breakup was mutual, on your initiative, or on your partner's initiative. Be with family and friends in your support network. Don't rush into another relationship. Depending on how involved you were with the partner you just broke up with, you may want to take a bit of a hiatus from dating. Regroup. At the same time, don't let the breakup spoil your enthusiasm for finding the right relationship for you.

If only we could do everything perfectly, without having to learn first! Life would be so easy. But that's not possible. We learn by doing. And in the course of doing, we often fail. Hopefully we learn from our failures and from our regrets and do better the next time.

To sum up, here are some basic dos and don'ts to make breaking up as smooth as possible:

- Don't break up in an email, a text, or even a phone call.

- Do put forth effort to make things work *before* you decide to break up.

- Do make a clean break (which doesn't preclude some contact at a future time).

- Don't engage in a blame game.

- Don't be too hard on yourself.

- Do take care of yourself afterward and prepare to move on with your life.

Having looked at how to end a relationship, we now turn to the more positive other side of the coin: how to take the next step beyond dating. In the next chapter, we look at how to formalize a new relationship to better ensure its long-term success.

CHAPTER 11

Making It Last

So you and your partner are still going strong, and feeling more and more positive as the days and weeks go by. You took the test in the last chapter, and it only confirmed what you already felt: you have no inclination or reason to even think about breaking up. In fact, everything you have learned and are continuing to learn about each other makes you more excited about your future together. It's all systems go.

Nor do you say this lightly. The two of you have really taken the time to get to know one another. You have vetted and sherlocked with due diligence, and enjoyed the process. You have learned to play together as well as to fight together. You can soothe and you can excite each other. You have formed a couple bubble, and feel safe and protected. In short, you are ready to take your relationship beyond dating!

This doesn't mean you won't continue to go on dates. Of course you will. What I'm talking about is moving beyond the initial dating relationship during which you get to know one another, and into a committed, long-term relationship. Some people may argue that there is no real distinction necessary between dating and a more committed relationship. They view it all as one flow, and react against inserting any point of initiation or ceremonial recognition as too arbitrary. I disagree. In fact, I think making a formal commitment in the form of a principle-based mutual agreement is an important step in the formation of a secure-functioning relationship.

You may be thinking that you fall into a middle group that is neither ready to break up nor all systems go for commitment. That's okay. You just need to spend more time vetting and getting to know each other. I said this process can take a year. But some people require longer, and that group could include you. Continue your exploration, with the goal of determining whether you and your potential partner are really moving toward secure functioning. Once you feel certain about that, you will probably also feel ready to make a commitment.

In this chapter, we will look at the reasons for making a specific and explicit commitment, as well as at several issues to address before you get there, and the kinds of agreements you and your partner can make. You will have a chance to walk through this process step by step, and craft your own couple pact.

WHY COMMIT

Throughout this book, I have been steering you toward a secure-functioning relationship. All the work you've done has been in the interest of developing a bond that is both satisfying and lasting beyond the early addictive phase of dating, when that cocktail of neurochemicals runs the show. Despite the thrill and enjoyment dopamine and its buddies generate, these chemicals have done nothing to help you build a sense of security. At this point in your relationship, and moving forward, you and your partner need to know you can count on one another. I believe that a formal agreement is the best way to set things up so you both reap the benefits of the security you have been building together.

Creating a couple pact is a sign of your maturity, integrity, and intelligence as partners. In the social sciences, these kinds of agreements are called *social contracts*. Going back—at least within modern times—to the seventeenth century, social contracts have enabled groups of people to join together under mutually agreed upon rules of social conduct. Placing each individual's well-being in line with the group's well-being allows everyone to enjoy greater health and happiness. Without a social agreement of any sort, we would live in a wild world indeed.

On a grand scale, within society as a whole, we could say social agreements are the work of society's ambassadors, who strive to gain control over the more primitive or warlike forces that threaten the peace. It is actually not so different at the level of your personal relationship. By this time, you and your partner have gotten to know both your primitives and your ambassadors. And you know who you want to be in charge. One of the main reasons to formally commit using a couple pact is to ensure that your ambassadors set the tone for your relationship. Your ambassadors' specialty is negotiating advantageous conditions for a relationship to endure. With their input, you can develop an agreement that lays down rules you can happily adhere to for now and into the future.

By the same token, if you choose not to develop a pact, you may put your relationship in jeopardy. Feelings and thoughts are like weather; they are constantly changing. If you operate solely according to your feelings in the moment, your relationship will be as unpredictable as the weather. You will hand over too much power to your primitives, and they probably won't act in ways that preserve your relationship when the going gets tough.

And there are other reasons to formally commit. In my view, the world can be an unpredictable, hostile, and unforgiving place. Coupling makes this reality more tolerable if you consider that two can be stronger than one. Couples who do not formally commit using principle-based mutual agreements are no more protected from the environment than they would be if they were single. Arguably, partners who remain in separate foxholes and create war on each other put themselves at greater risk for stress and anxiety.

As we established at the beginning of this book, there are no absolutes when it comes to relationships. What kind of partnership you want to be in, or even whether you want to be in a partnership at all, is a choice for you to make. However, if you decide you want to be in a secure-functioning relationship, then eventually you reach a point where voluntarily surrendering to another person is the next most meaningful step. You make this commitment recognizing it as a transcendent investment in your mutual safety and benefit. To a wave or an island, the idea of surrender to another person probably sounds like a prison sentence or, at a minimum, like throwing oneself under the bus. Hopefully, having followed the process I have laid out so far, you no longer find yourself driven by fears or cynicism, and instead are ready and eager to take a leap forward with your chosen partner.

MAKING THE AGREEMENT

Remember Warren and Sue, the anchor couple who met at a summer youth service camp? Here's how things turned out for them. Within two months of their first date, they had begun sleeping together and met each other's families. Each said they were falling for the other. Before going to the camp, Sue had casually dated a neighbor of hers; now she told Warren she wanted them to see each other exclusively. At this point, they decided to create their first couple pact. It focused on establishing exclusivity and made explicit their desire to explore their partnership and see where it would go. It included these terms, among others:

- We agree to date one another only.

- We agree to discuss and reassess the terms of our new commitment, as needed.

- We promise to be fully honest about our feelings, whether negative or positive.

- I, Sue, promise to have fun and enjoy you, Warren.

- I, Warren, promise to have fun and enjoy you, Sue.

Sue and Warren initially had a lighthearted attitude about their couple pact. In fact, the first time Sue referred to the two of them as a "couple," Warren quipped, "Yeah, a couple of lovesick fools!" However, both took the pact seriously, and about six months later they began talking about marriage. They eventually decided to live together for a year before making the ultimate commitment. Sue didn't want to consider living together a formal engagement, but on her birthday, after they had lived together successfully for some months, Warren proposed, and she accepted. Throughout this time, the couple added to their pact.

When they wrote their wedding vows, Sue and Warren included many of the statements from the pact. To this day, they like revising and adding elements to it. One recent addition was "We agree to share this pregnancy as if we both are carrying this child for nine months."

Jennifer and Bradley (the island who was easily distracted by other people on their first date at a restaurant) used their couple pact somewhat differently. This couple dated for two years before they decided to become engaged. Although they had sex, they never considered living together before marriage. When Bradley proposed, Jennifer was eager to accept. The couple had come a long way in terms of their ability to negotiate differences in their relationship styles. However, Jennifer wanted to be more confident that they could do this successfully in marriage. So she asked Bradley if they could develop a couple pact. Bradley was initially resistant because he envisioned a lengthy engagement and was afraid Jennifer would use a pact to pen him in. However, he was motivated to get an affirmative answer to his proposal, so he agreed.

Many of the terms Jennifer and Bradley wrote focused on addressing communication issues they had encountered and on ensuring mutuality going forward. For example:

- We agree to bring all issues to the table promptly, and never go to sleep before we are both feeling comfortable and secure with each other.

- We agree to always hear each other out, without interruption.

- We agree to give each other the benefit of the doubt.

- We agree to always give one another a second chance.

- We agree to negotiate time to talk, rather than spring intense conversations on each other.

This agreement helped Jennifer and Bradley have a successful engagement, and they married eighteen months later. Although they did not make their pact part of the wedding ceremony, they continue to develop it as a married couple. Often, they use it as part of their strategy to manage issues that come up, adding terms specific to their current situation. They understand that it represents the basic operating principles of their relationship, and appreciate that they can reword the terms when necessary. For example, Bradley proposed they say: "We agree to leave all messes created in the family room untouched for at least two days." After discussion, this was revised to a more neutral principle: "We balance our support for each other's creativity with respect for our mutual needs."

Carrie and Evan, the waves who fought over whether to stay together in the motel on their first out-of-town date, became engaged after only nine months. Both wanted desperately to make the relationship work. Nevertheless, by the one year anniversary of their first date, they were floundering. They sought the help of a couple therapist, who during the course of their work suggested a formal couple agreement. The terms focused heavily on how they could provide security for one another. For example:

- We agree to stand by one another. Standing together, we are stronger than whatever the world throws at us.

- We will never allow our pasts to overshadow our present together.

- We will never use our words as weapons, but instead heal each other with hugs.

We see from these examples that while couple pacts have the same basic purpose, they can vary in terms of when and how couples develop and apply them. A pact can be formed relatively early in your relationship or can come as part of your marriage vows. It can and should be tailored to the specific needs and dynamics of your relationship. In other words, although pacts may share common elements, there is no one-size-fits-all couple agreement. You and your partner must work together to craft one that is meaningful for both of you.

YOUR MUTUAL COMMANDMENTS

I did not invent the idea of couple agreements, so you may run across descriptions for creating them in the media and in books. Many of these focus on practical demands between partners, such as how much sex they expect, ownership of pets, management of finances, and so on. In fact, an increasing number of law firms these days offer couple contracts. To be clear, I am not talking about these kinds of agreements. From a psychobiological perspective, a couple pact lays out the set of operating principles for your secure-functioning relationship.

You can think of a couple pact as being a bit like your own set of Ten Commandments—pithy laws you both buy into and that serve both of you and the relationship itself. These laws should capture what is truly important not just now, but ideally for years to come. This is not to say you have to come up with exactly ten, or that you can't revise and add to your pact.

The language you use is important. I suggest something that sounds similar to "This is what we agree to do…and this is what we agree not to do." In this way, your pact will differ from the Ten Commandments, which use moralizing language to dictate "You *should* not do this!" You don't want your pact to hang like a sledge-hammer over your heads. Nor do you want to ever use the pact against each other. Rather, it represents your mutual desires and aspirations for your relationship.

PACT EXAMPLES

The following are some items that have worked well for other couples and that you can take as examples when developing your own couple pact.

- We tell each other everything; we aim for complete transparency.

- We are the first to know and never the last. We are each other's go-to people and give each other all important information first.

- We have access to one another twenty-four hours a day, seven days a week, without complaint.

- We protect each other in public and private.

- We agree to be experts on one another and have each other's owner's manual.

- We agreed to be even better at our relationship than we are at our jobs.

- We are the gatekeepers of all things, ideas, tasks, and people that wish to intrude on our couple bubble and compete for our valuable resources.

- We never throw each other under the bus or relegate the other to third wheel status.

- We agree to take care of personal and mutual distress as fast as reasonably possible, putting relief before all other things, such as being right.

- We agree to repair any known injuries as fast as possible, in a way that relieves our partner.

- We are dedicated to the principle of maintaining a truly mutual relationship based on fairness, justice, and sensitivity.

- We agree to never threaten the relationship itself because we understand the perils that come with such a tactic.

- We agree to pay special attention to our own threatening gestures, vocal patterns, facial expressions, movements, and dangerous phrases that may lead either of us to feel threatened, and thereby harm our mutual safety and security.

EXERCISE: CREATING YOUR COUPLE PACT

All the other exercises in this book can be done without the directly acknowledged involvement of your partner. This one, however, is predicated on your mutual involvement. You might be the one suggesting the creation of a formal agreement, but it must represent the equal effort of both partners.

A word of caution. Island and wave partners may be hesitant when it comes to creating a couple pact. This is usually a reflection of their general reluctance to commit. Seeing the elements of commitment literally "in writing" can feed into their fears or defenses. If this is the case, I suggest proceeding with caution. Stressing the buy-in phase can help an island or wave feel more comfortable. And know that islands and waves have the ability to make and keep commitments, including ones spelled out in a couple pact.

1. **Preliminary discussion.** First, I suggest you and your partner get together and discuss the idea of a couple pact. Talk about what it means to you and how it could benefit your relationship. It is important that you both acknowledge your readiness to engage in this process before you actually begin.

2. **Formulate your pact.** I suggest using a brainstorming process whereby you come up with a range of principles you could include. Allow yourselves the freedom to be creative, without initial censorship. You will have time for that later. Aim for succinct statements that are clear and would be easy to follow. Items should resonate with both partners, and be stated in a way that either can hold the other to when a breach of an agreed upon principle occurs.

3. **Get buy-in.** Go over all the statements you have come up with and decide which you want to include in your couple pact. This is the time to make any revisions. Keep working on each item until you either are happy with it or reject it. Remember, both of you have to agree upon all items if they are to be included in your pact. You can print it out and actually sign it. You may want to post it somewhere you both can view it easily.

4. **Design your celebration.** Many couples like to officially inaugurate their pact. It could be something as simple as drinking a toast or going out for dinner. Or your pact could be incorporated into marriage vows or another form of relationship vows.

5. **Moving forward.** Unlike marriage vows, which are "till death do us part," couple pacts can be revised. Let it grow with your relationship. You may find agreements you had not thought of before or were not yet ready to make, or better ways to state agreements you initially created.

LIVING TOGETHER

One issue many couples wish to consider before they form their couple pact is whether to live together before getting married or making another form of long-term commitment. Arguments can be made both for and against. Both options are equally valid; ultimately, the choice is up to you.

Personally, I favor living together prior to a long-term commitment, provided both partners are okay with this. Living together allows you to learn more about each other and what it is like to live with this person on a day-to-day basis. Dates and honeymoons and vacations can tell you only so much. Your relationship is more likely to succeed if you have a better sense of what it's like to be with your partner in a real living situation, rather than taking the risk of discovering that after you have married or made a long-term commitment.

Of course, there will always be things you find out later. We all have our share of unknowns, mysteries, and secrets, some of which are unknown even to us. One of the joys of relationship is the opportunity it provides to learn more about each other throughout life. Nevertheless, the argument for living together is that you are able to maximize the amount you know about each other and minimize the risk of making a commitment you will later regret. In this case, my suggestion is to create a couple pact that works for living together, and then adapt it as needed if and when your relationship progresses from there.

BREACH OF CONTRACT

I would like to say this will never happen. But it will and does, in small ways and large. Obviously, large breaches are a sign you may not be ready for a long-term commitment or that this person is not the right partner for you after all. If this is the case, be thankful that you created an agreement early on that allowed you to find this out and make changes before you further cemented your relationship. And from there, it's back to chapter 10. Sorry!

On the other hand, small breaches may be a sign that you need to revise a term in the agreement. Perhaps it was not sufficiently principle based. Or perhaps you did not both buy in to it, even if you thought you did. There could be many reasons here, but the good news is that you can work to further clarify the agreements you made. The irony is that a breach is actually a good thing in this case because it sheds light on the areas you and your partner need to clarify and fix.

I urge you, however, to try not to punish each other for any breach, even if you are tempted to do so. Punishment will not move you closer to secure functioning. Instead, consult the agreement(s) you made that indicates how you want to go about resolving any conflicts between you. If you don't yet have any such agreements, this would be a good time to clarify the principles you want to follow and add this to your couple pact.

FINAL THOUGHTS

This chapter marks the end of one era and the beginning of a new one. The vetting period officially ends when you marry or make a long-term commitment. It's not fair to continue auditioning each other when you've already made your choice. Now you will continue to learn about each other, but you will no longer use what you learn as the basis for making a decision about whether this is the right partner for you.

Here are some dos and don'ts for making a couple pact:

- Do make it a fully collaborative process.

- Do use simple, straightforward language.

- Do be creative and have fun creating your pact.

- Do focus on making agreements that foster the principle of secure functioning.

- Don't use the pact or any part of it to coerce your partner.

- Don't treat your pact as static or not open to revision or improvement.

- Do make every effort under heaven to adhere to the agreements you make.

CHAPTER 12

Dating Is Forever

One of the things I ask couples in a long-term committed relationship who come to me for help is whether they are still girlfriend and boyfriend (or boyfriend and boyfriend, and so on, as the case may be). Many are surprised by the question.

"What do you mean, are we still girlfriend and boyfriend?" one partner asks. "We're married. We're beyond all that now."

This is a common notion, and I believe it is a mistake. Even when you're in a committed relationship, I believe you should remain in dating mode, at least to some degree. It's the dating mode that helps create novelty, excitement, and the desirable kind of strangerness we talked about in chapter 2.

Tracey and I continue to date one another. Our dating experience is mostly related to travel, especially since we founded the PACT Institute to train therapists to use the kinds of psychobiological techniques that are the basis of this book. We travel constantly to training sites, both around the country and internationally, and love seeing new sights and meeting new people.

Traveling, for us, is a team process. We have traveling down to a science. One thing we have learned (thank you, Tracey) is to pack using carry-ons only, even when going to faraway places for long periods. We share leadership roles. Tracey is "Scout" and I'm "Tracker." Because we both love people, we meet folks on planes and trains, and often in the strangest of places. It seems that wherever we go, something unexpected happens, from the sublime to the ridiculous.

On one occasion—in this case, not a business trip—we were strolling the beach in Waikiki, going from hotel to hotel. We came across an outdoor dance party and spontaneously decided to join in. While dancing, we noticed that everyone else was wearing a yellow lei. We asked another dancing couple, and we were told the dancers were all involved in a remarriage ceremony. Almost before we knew it, we had both been given yellow leis and found ourselves getting married all over again.

I'm not suggesting that you need to travel in order to keep your relationship fresh and in dating mode. Anything you do that is novel or adventuresome can put you back in dating mode. The ambassadors crave newness, and a surefire way to experience that newness is by bringing each other into novel adventures.

Tracey and I push each other to do things that we otherwise might not do. Often this includes the art of negotiation. For example, one evening Tracey wanted to have a drink at our favorite haunt, and I wanted to see a movie. You would only have needed the most basic sherlocking skills to recognize that I'm not a fan of going out just for drinks, and to discover that Tracey prefers activities that allow us to give each other more attention. So what did we do? We ended up going to the movie first, and having a drink afterward to talk about the movie. We both won, and also both did something we didn't like.

I'm sharing a bit of my own experience to illustrate some of the ways in which a relationship is always an adventure, always in development. I don't care how "beyond all that" you think you are; partners can and will get on each other's nerves. They fight about stupid stuff. They say things they wish they hadn't said. They have bad days.

But that shouldn't scare you. You now have sherlocking and mindfulness skills, and know how to work with each other's nervous systems. You have dispelled many common myths about love relationships. You are aware of behaviors that result from anchor, island,

and wave tendencies and know how to respond most effectively. You know the importance of creating a couple bubble, of protecting each other in public and in private, and of taking each other's distress seriously and ministering to each other as soon as possible. In short, there is some hard work to be done, but you have the tools to do it.

When I say that dating is forever, I don't mean in any way to discourage you or give the impression you will never reach your relationship goals. In fact, just the opposite. I encourage you to take what you have learned here and not just apply it for a few months or years of dating, but bring it into your long-term relationship. Let it be a lesson that keeps on giving. Use it to make sure your relationship flourishes. Dating can be one of the most enjoyable and exciting things you'll ever do. So buckle up—and happy dating!

Acknowlegments

First I must acknowledge my editor and dear friend, Jude Berman, who has kept me going and writing when my own avoidance and island nature take over. And as I've said before, I stand on the shoulders of my mentors who I have channeled all these years: Allan Schore, James Masterson, Marion Solomon, Stephen Porges, Harville Hendrix, and John Gottman, to name just a few.

I also want to thank from the bottom of my heart people whom I love and adore, starting with Helen LaKelly Hunt, who co-wrote the foreword with Harville Hendrix; Helen Fisher; Lou Cozolino; Dan Siegel; Ellyn Bader; Pete Pearson; Pat Ogden; Pat Love; Jeffrey Zeig; Bill O'Hanlon; Dan Wile; and of course Alanis Morissette.

References

Ainsworth, M. D. S., S. M. Bell, and D. J. Stayton. 1971. "Individual Differences in Strange-Situational Behaviour of One-Year-Olds." In *The Origins of Human Social Relations*, edited by H. R. Schaffer. New York: Academic Press.

Bowlby, J. 1969. *Attachment and Loss*. New York: Basic Books.

Brazelton, T. B. 1992. *Touchpoints: Your Child's Emotional and Behavioral Development*. Reading, MA: Perseus Books.

Desilver, D. 2014. "5 Facts About Love and Marriage." *Fact Tank*. Retrieved from http://www.pewresearch.org/fact-tank/2014/02/14/5-facts-about-love-and-marriage/

Ditzen, B., U. M. Nater, M. Schaer, R. La Marca, G. Bodenmann, U. Ehlert, and M. Heinrichs. 2013. "Sex-Specific Effects of Intranasal Oxytocin on Autonomic Nervous System and Emotional Responses to Couple Conflict." *Social Cognitive and Affective Neuroscience* 8(8):897–902. doi:10.1093/scan/nss083

Fisher, H. E., A. Aron, D. Mashek, H. Li, and L. L. Brown. 2002. "Defining the Brain Systems of Lust, Romantic Attraction and Attachment." *Archives of Sexual Behavior* 31(5):413–9.

Fisher, H. E., L. L. Brown, A. Aron, G. Strong, and D. Mashek. 2010. "Reward, Addiction, and Emotion Regulation Systems Associated with Rejection in Love. *Journal of Neurophysiology* 104(1):51–60.

Hazan, C., and P. Shaver. "Romantic Love Conceptualized as an Attachment Process. 1987. *Journal of Personality and Social Psychology* 52:511–24.

Hendrix, H. 2007. *Getting the Love You Want: A Guide for Couples*. New York: Henry Holt.

Lutz, J., et al. 2014. "Mindfulness and Emotion Regulation: An fMRI Study." *Social Cognitive and Affective Neuroscience* 9(6):776–85.

Marazziti, D., H. S. Akiskal, A. Rossi, and G. B. Cassano. 1999. "Alteration of the Platelet Serotonin Transporter in Romantic Love. *Psychological Medicine* 29(3):741–5.

Marazziti, D., and S. Baroni. 2012. "Romantic Love: The Mistery of Its Biological Roots." *Clinical Neuropsychiatry* 9(1):14–19.

Mickelson, K. D., R. C. Kessler, and P. R. Shaver. "Adult Attachment in a Nationally Representative Sample." 1997. *Journal of Personality and Social Psychology* 73(5):1092–106.

Moreland, R. L., and R. B. Zajonc. 1982. "Exposure Effects in Person Perception: Familiarity, Similarity, and Attraction." *Journal of Experimental Social Psychology* 18:395–415.

Moullin, S., J. Waldfogel, and E. Washbrook. 2014. *Baby Bonds: Parenting, Attachment and a Secure Base for Children.* London: The Sutton Trust.

Parrott, L., and L. Parrott. 2013. *The Good Fight: How Conflict Can Bring You Closer.* Brentwood, TN: Worthy Publishing.

Perrett, D. I., K. A. Mai, and S. Yoshikawa. 1994. "Facial Shapes and Judgments of Female Attractiveness." *Nature* 368:239–42.

Phillips, R. 2013. Uninterrupted Skin-to-Skin Contact Immediately After Birth. *Newborn and Infant Nursing Reviews* 13(2):67–72.

Porges, S. W. 2009. "Reciprocal Influences Between Body and Brain in the Perception and Expression of Affect: A Polyvagal Perspective. In *The Healing Power of Emotion: Affective Neuroscience, Development, and Clinical Practice,* edited by D. Fosha, D. Siegel, and M. Solomon. New York: Norton.

Porges, S. W. 2011. *The Polyvagal Theory: Neurophysiological Foundations of Emotions, Attachment, Communication, and Self-Regulation.* New York: Norton.

Princeton University, Woodrow Wilson School of Public and International Affairs. 2014. "Four in 10 Infants Lack Strong Parental Attachments. *ScienceDaily.* Retrieved from www.sciencedaily.com/releases/2014/03 /140327123540.htm

Reis, H. T., M. R. Maniaci, P. A. Caprariello, P. W. Eastwick, and E. J. Finkel. 2011. "Familiarity Does Indeed Promote Attraction in Live Interaction. *Journal of Personality and Social Psychology* 101:557–70.

Schore, A. N. 2002. *Affect Regulation and Repair of the Self.* New York: Norton.

Siegel, D. J. 2007. *The Mindful Brain: Reflection and Attunement in the Cultivation of Well-Being.* New York: Norton.

Smith, A., and M. Duggan. 2013. "Online Dating & Relationships." *Pew Research Internet Project*. Retrieved from http://www.pewinternet.org/2013/10/21/online-dating-relationships/

Statistic Brain. 2014. *Online Dating Statistics*. Retrieved from http://www.statisticbrain.com/online-dating-statistics/

Tatkin, S. 2012. *Wired for Love: How Understanding Your Partner's Brain Can Help You Defuse Conflicts and Spark Intimacy*. Oakland, CA: New Harbinger Publications.

Tessina, T. 2008. *Money, Sex, and Kids: Stop Fighting about the Three Things That Can Ruin Your Marriage*. Avon, MA: Adams Media.

Stan Tatkin, PsyD, MFT, is the author of *Wired for Love* and *Your Brain on Love*, and coauthor of *Love and War in Intimate Relationships*. He has a clinical practice in Southern California, teaches at Kaiser Permanente, and is assistant clinical professor at the University of California, Los Angeles. Tatkin developed the Psychobiological Approach to Couple Therapy® (PACT), and together with his wife Tracey Boldemann-Tatkin, founded the PACT Institute.

Foreword writers **Harville Hendrix, PhD**, and **Helen LaKelly Hunt, PhD**, are partners in life and work. They cocreated Imago relationship therapy (IRT); cofounded Imago Relationships International, Inc., which supports Imago couples therapists in thirty-seven countries; and have written several books on intimate relationships, including Hendrix's *New York Times* bestseller *Getting the Love You Want*, which has been published in sixty languages. Hendrix appeared on *Oprah* seventeen times. Hunt was inducted into the National Women's Hall of Fame.

MORE BOOKS *from*
NEW HARBINGER PUBLICATIONS

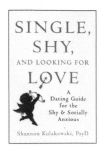

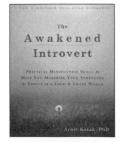